To Helen

Sarah

Rachel x

MILLINERY

THE ART OF HAT-MAKING

SARAH LOMAX & RACHEL SKINNER

A NOTE ON MEASUREMENTS
The imperial measurements in these
projects are converted from metric.
While every attempt has been made
to ensure that they are as accurate as
possible, some rounding up or down
has been inevitable. For this reason,
it is always best to keep to one system
or the other throughout a project:
do not mix metric and imperial units.

First published 2017 by
Guild of Master Craftsman Publications Ltd
Castle Place, 166 High Street, Lewes,
East Sussex, BN7 1XU

Text © Sarah Lomax and Rachel Skinner, 2017
Copyright in the Work © GMC Publications Ltd, 2017

Step-by-step photography by Sarah Lomax and Rachel Skinner

ISBN 978 1 78494 354 7

A catalogue record for this book is available from the British Library.

Publisher Jonathan Bailey
Production Manager Jim Bulley
Senior Project Editor Dominique Page
Editor Judith Chamberlain
Managing Art Editor Gilda Pacitti
Designer Luana Gobbo
Photographer Neal Grundy
Styling Wayne Blades

Colour origination by GMC Reprographics
Printed and bound in Turkey

"*I myself have twelve hats, and each one represents a different personality. Why just be yourself?*"

MARGARET ATWOOD
Novelist

BRIDAL
HEADDRESS
PAGE 136

FELT CAPELINE
PAGE 44

FEATHER HAIRBAND
PAGE 58

FELT TRILBY
PAGE 82

SPARKLING
COCKTAIL HAT
PAGE 108

SCULPTED
SINAMAY
PAGE 126

MAGENTA
PERCHER
PAGE 36

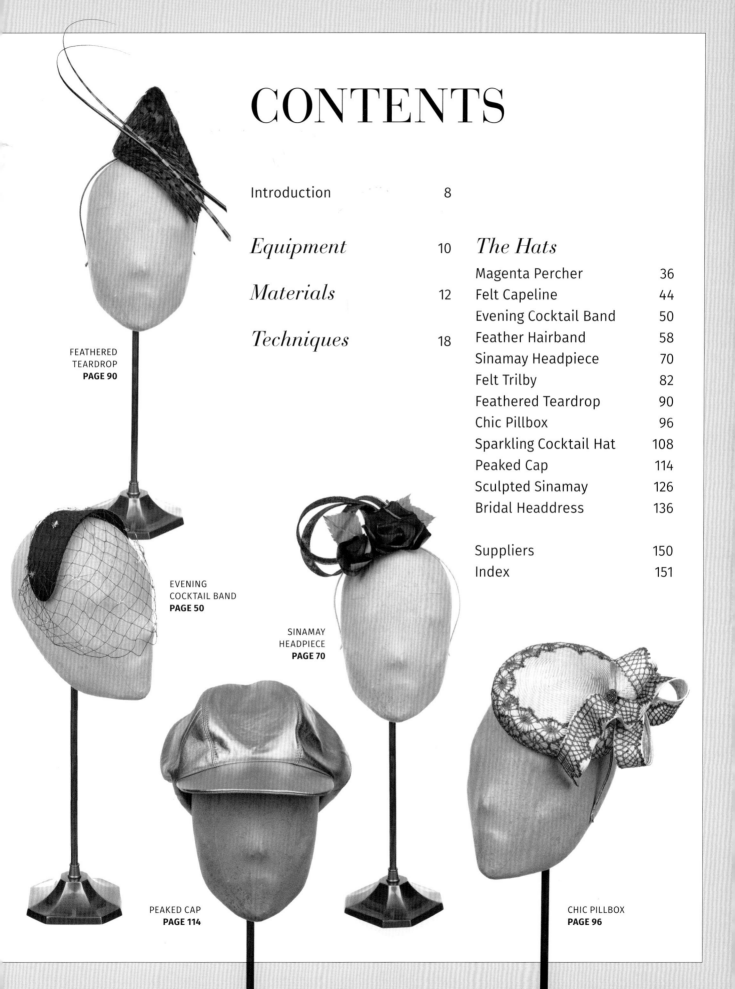

CONTENTS

FEATHERED
TEARDROP
PAGE 90

EVENING
COCKTAIL BAND
PAGE 50

SINAMAY
HEADPIECE
PAGE 70

PEAKED CAP
PAGE 114

CHIC PILLBOX
PAGE 96

INTRODUCTION

W EARING A HAT CAN TURN AN OCCASION INTO
SOMETHING REALLY SPECIAL. Hats can conjure up many
feelings and emotions – they are not only practical, they are about
escapism and being someone else. Whereas in the past, fashion
dictated what kind of hats people wore and when they wore them,
never has there been a better time to enjoy wearing hats simply
for the pleasure of it.

This book distils over 50 years of our joint experience of designing,
creating and making hats. Millinery gives us the opportunity to use
our hands to combine art, craft, sculpture and fashion. The variations
on style, fabric choice, colour and trims are endless and we love using
luxurious, beautiful materials to create something truly marvellous
– a three-dimensional artwork that can really finish off any outfit.

We both loved sewing and making things as children, and after art
and fashion colleges we were lucky to get apprenticeships with
Frederick Fox, who was the Queen's milliner for more than 35 years.
As students there we received one-on-one intensive teaching.
We learned to be incredibly thorough and work to a very high
standard, as you would expect since we were making hats for the
Royal Family. It was a privilege to learn these skills and our aim in this
book is to pass on these traditional techniques and keep them alive.

Creativity is involved at every stage and we teach you what we have learned and what we are still learning. At the beginning of the book we outline the equipment and materials that you will need. There are many different methods of making hats but in our techniques section we have listed the skills that we use most often and which are in these projects. Some projects are designed for the absolute beginner, while other projects will attract and challenge the more experienced milliner.

In this book we want to share our love of millinery. Designing and creating hats is very individual and every milliner has his or her own way of working. It takes years of experience to build up the skills needed and reach perfection. Our experience is that millinery can be mindful and therapeutic, rewarding and enjoyable. We want you to be inspired and enjoy making these projects as much as we've had fun creating them for you.

Happy hat-making!

Sarah and Rachel

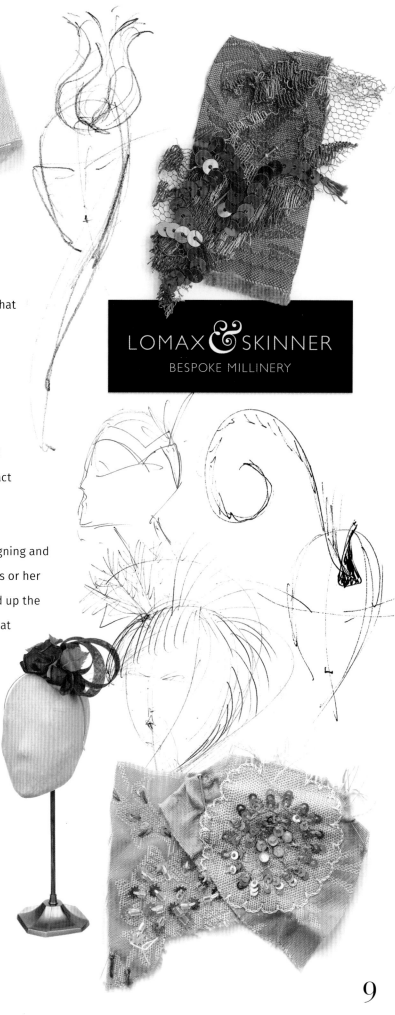

LOMAX & SKINNER
BESPOKE MILLINERY

EQUIPMENT

THE BASIC KIT

Much of the equipment used in millinery can be found around the home. You will be able to go a long way with a basic dressmaker's kit and a household kettle and iron. A sewing machine is useful but not essential. There are, however, a few items of equipment outside of the basic kit that will be needed as you explore millinery more.

Thimble
Apart from a tape measure, a thimble is one of the most essential items of equipment. It is needed when blocking to push pins into wooden blocks but also when sewing through layers of materials.

Pliers and scissors
You will need pliers with a cutting edge for cutting and manipulating wire. A good-quality pair of jewellery-making pliers would be perfect, and ideally you would have three pairs of scissors: one pair of cutting shears with long, sharp blades for use with fabrics; one pair for cutting paper, buckram, sinamays and straws; and a small pair of embroidery scissors for intricate work and snipping threads.

Needles and pins
We couldn't manage without good-quality needles and pins. Our favourite needles are a 'Milliners Straw'. They come in different sizes but we like a no. 7. It is a good, long needle that is tough enough for the heavy sewing sometimes required of it but thin enough for delicate fabrics.

You will need short, strong, flat-ended pins for blocking and longer, finer pins for the silks, laces and delicate fabrics.

Nylon cord
A strong nylon cord, known as a blocking cord, is extremely useful. It is used alongside pins for securing materials and fabrics when blocking and during the drying process.

Clothes brush
Also useful is a small clothes brush. We use ours alongside steam from the kettle for lifting the pile of a velour felt after blocking to give it a nice finish.

Corsetry boning / long palette knife
For easing blocked shapes off the block, a piece of corsetry boning or a long palette knife is very handy.

Iron and pressing cloths
Your household iron and ironing board will be in constant use while working on projects. There will be ironing of flat fabrics in preparation, and pressing at stages of the project that will often be required to be done in the hand. A pressing pad held under the work will allow you to use an iron safely in the hand. This pad should be made from several layers of fabric such as a tea towel. It should be bulky enough to keep the heat well away from your hand and have a smooth surface to ensure a good finish.

Use a pressing cloth between the iron and the surface you are pressing to avoid any marks or dirt transferring from the iron to your work. A piece of cotton fabric will be more than suitable for pressing felts but it could stick to stiffened straws and sinamays, leaving fibres behind. A small piece of organza or non-stick paper is ideal for these fabrics.

> ### HEALTH AND SAFETY
> Appropriate care and caution should always be taken when working with hot irons, steam, chemical stiffeners and glues, and any sharp tools.

HAT BLOCKS

Wooden hat blocks are a thing of beauty and all milliners are proud of their collection. Back in our early days of millinery we would scour charity shops and antique markets for old blocks, and many interesting shapes could be found at a reasonable cost. These days they are becoming more and more difficult to find, but it is always worth keeping your eyes open!

Block making is a specialized trade that has significantly diminished over the last 50 years or so, but there are still a few small companies of talented block makers keeping milliners supplied. They sell all the popular and useful shapes 'off the shelf' but they will also make blocks to your own designs.

When starting out it won't be necessary to buy a large variety of blocks but a domed crown block will be an investment worth making. With a little imagination and experimentation, you will be able to use it for a variety of shapes, and even sizes. One of the many things we love about millinery is being inventive with our blocks and the more experience you have of millinery the more you will learn to improvise and see shapes in what you have at your disposal.

Blocking does not have to be restricted to only being done on wooden blocks. As long as you have an object that is strong enough to withstand the pulling of millinery materials, and the material can be secured while drying, you can use it. One of our most popular hats was blocked on a quiche tin! Search the house for items such as bowls or bread boards that could be used, or consider items from craft shops, such as polystyrene balls, that could become your next beautiful hat.

A poupee or dolly head is a calico-covered head mannequin that's extremely useful for working out proportions and arranging trimmings when designing. It can also be used for setting petersham ribbon in the head fit for a professional finish. You will not need a poupee for any of the projects in this book but if you decided to take your millinery further, it would be an excellent piece of equipment to have that will last you forever.

A collection of different shapes of hat blocks, including the domed crown top (top right).

Poupee or dolly heads are useful when working on hats but are not essential.

MATERIALS

FOUNDATION MATERIALS

A number of different factors will inform your choice of foundation for your fabric-covered project, and this isn't a comprehensive list of the materials available – rather the ones we favour and most often use. As a general rule, the heavier the fabric, the heavier the foundation material needs to be. But when choosing your foundation you will also need to give careful consideration to the style of hat you are making and its finished weight. Hats should always be kept as light as possible.

Buckram (A)
Millinery buckram is a widely available and very versatile white or black cotton woven fabric that is impregnated with starch. It can be used to create hats from flat patterns, or when steamed it will soften, allowing you to shape it over a hat block or manipulate it with your hands. When dry it will retain the shape you have created.

It is available in different weights and stiffness, and choosing the correct one will depend on the style of hat and the facing fabric being used. Throughout the projects we have used a single, stiffened, medium-weight buckram.

Paris, Dior or blocking net (B)
Paris, Dior or blocking net is a stiffened cotton fabric, also available in black and white, and known by any of its three names. Because it is knitted rather than woven it is less dense than buckram, making it easier to block although still retaining its shape when dry. However, it is only really suitable for lighter weight fabrics and the smaller types of hats and headpieces.

Felts and straws (C)
Felts and straws can also be very effective lightweight foundations for material-covered hats (see page 14 for more information on these materials).

Other materials
Although not strictly foundation fabrics, the materials listed below have been included because they go hand-in-hand with the foundation material to soften its look and to prevent glue from coming through to the right side of the work.

Domette (D) is a soft, 100% cotton material that is available either in a fusible or non-fusible form. It is perfect for use with lightweight silks and cottons to give a beautiful, luxurious finish.

Fusible interlining (E) is widely available as a cotton or synthetic material in black or white. It is used to give body to fine fabrics and to prevent glue seeping through to the right side of the work.

Tarlatan (F) is a lightweight, non-fusible, 100% cotton interfacing that is also slightly stiffened. We mainly use it to give a smooth finish to a wired edge but its stiffness makes it ideal for pattern making.

Adhesive web (G) is a strong, paper-backed, heat-reactive web of glue. It is especially useful for bonding fine fabrics such as silks and lace.

FABRICS AND TRIMMINGS

The incredible array of beautiful materials and trimmings in fabric shops can be overwhelming, but you will soon discover your favourite materials to work with. We particularly love working with silk dupion, satins, lace and organza.

All materials, with the exception of straws and felts, are used on the bias. Material cut on the bias is used extensively in millinery, as it is where the stretch of the fabric is found – the straight grain of the fabric is firm with little or no movement in it. You need the stretch for blocking and moulding flat materials, but it is also essential for many other techniques in millinery, such as draping, making rouleaux, shaping petals for flowers, and tip and side band linings to name but a few.

To find the true cross of a piece of material, fold one corner over so that the exact grain of the weft (the width of the material from selvedge to selvedge) is at right angles to the warp (the length of the material). The diagonal formed is the bias, and the width of any bias strip needed should be accurately measured from this diagonal.

Felt (**A**)

Felts are made of loose, fur fibres matted together under pressure and steam. There is no straight of grain, and when they are warm and damp they can be stretched and manipulated in any direction and will hold their shape when dry. There are many different types of felt to choose from, ranging greatly in cost and quality. Some come with elaborate printed patterns, which can make for very striking hats.

Felts come in three sizes or shapes called cones or hoods, flares and capelines. Cones or hoods are used for crowns and small shapes, and capelines and flares are used for a larger crown and brim shape.

Straw (**B**)

Like felts, there's a huge variety of straws available in different shapes and sizes – too many to describe in great detail. We favour parasisal straw for the majority of our work because of its high quality. It's a fine natural straw with a smooth weave made from the fibres of the sisal plant that take dye well.

Sinamay (C)

We also use sinamay, which is a flat fabric woven from the processed stalks of the abaca tree – a banana palm that is native to the Philippines. With its strong nature and stretch on the bias, it is a very popular material for millinery and, once stiffened, keeps its shape well. It has an open weave and is used in layers, depending on the translucency and strength needed. Because it's a natural fibre, it holds colour beautifully if you are dyeing it at home, but it can also be purchased in a huge array of colours. Many different qualities, weaves, grades and textures are available.

Feathers (D)

Feathers are intricate to work with and extremely decorative. They dye well and it can be satisfying cutting and curling them into fantastical shapes and twists. Individual plumes and quills, bundles, pre-made elaborate mounts and fringes of feathers are all readily available from suppliers. It's also fun to collect feathers from the ground when you're out for a walk. Washing and preparing them can be time consuming but it's worth it. In Victorian times, part of a milliner's work was to dissect a whole bird, treat it with chemicals and carefully put it back together again. It would be quite an elaborate and heavy embellishment to a lady's hat. Thankfully, it's no longer fashionable!

Flowers (E)

Flowers have always been popular in millinery. There is a huge amount of choice, whether you are buying them direct from a hand-crafted flower maker, sourcing them from a department store or making your own to be individual and to match the hat. Light silks for summer flowers and velvets for winter flowers always brighten up any style.

Veiling (F)

Veiling adds softness. It's pretty and feminine, chic and mysterious. It should be worked with a light hand, as if it has just floated onto the hat. It is readily available with fine and delicate patterns or bolder designs with chenille spots. It can be blocked, gathered, cut and draped onto the hat.

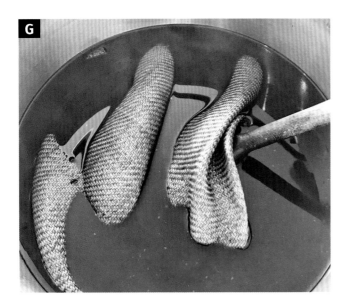

Dyes (G)

It is useful to build up a selection of coloured dyes. If you're making bespoke hats, you may need to match the hats with outfits. It's worth experimenting with colours, as many of the trimmings and materials can be dyed first before making up.

Wire (H)

Millinery wire is a cotton-covered copper wire that is available in different gauges. The millinery wire that we find most suitable for the majority of our work is a US 16 gauge (SWG 18, 1.2mm) wire. We also often use a US 26 gauge (SWG 27, 0.4mm) wire, which is almost thread-like and excellent for flower stems, creating veining in leaves and securing trimmings.

Vintage finds (I)

A lovely part of our work is visiting markets for interesting vintage finds that can then make your creation unique and one of a kind. Pieces of old jewellery, brooches and buttons can make for an eye-catching detail on a hat.

Petersham ribbon (J)

Petersham is a grosgrain ribbon. It comes in many colours and different widths. As well as making the perfect band and trimming around a hat, it is also used for the head fitting inside hats.

STIFFENERS

Choosing the correct stiffener for your project, and environment, will require research, and your own favourites will become clear after practice and experience. All materials vary in quality and some won't need any stiffening, but it's often necessary to stiffen felts either before or after they have been blocked, and most straws will require some stiffening to help retain a good shape and give a nice finish. When you are creating trims out of fabric these will also often need to be stiffened, too.

There are two main types of stiffener: a chemical one and a water-based one. You should make sure you check the safety data information supplied for correct usage and do a small sample test. The water-based stiffener can be applied with brushes or sponges and needs to be worked well into the material you are stiffening. The brushes or sponges can be cleaned after use with water. Felts and others fabrics treated with water-based stiffeners are most often left to dry before working in the steam. Chemical stiffeners for both straws and felts are available. They will need to be used alongside thinners and with appropriate caution.

Generally, you apply felt stiffener using a brush to the inside of a crown or the underside of a brim, often after it has come off the block. The chemical straw stiffener is also applied with a brush, evenly and sparingly, once the blocked hat is dry but still on the block. Brushes that have been used for chemical stiffeners will need to be cleaned with thinners.

We also find a good-quality, firm-hold hairspray very useful as a stiffener, particularly on fine silks and laces. It will only give a low level of stiffness that can disappear if the material is over-worked, but it has the advantage of not changing the character of the fabric, which some other stiffeners can do.

TECHNIQUES

STITCHES

Listed below are the stitches we use all the time and consider essential to millinery. If it's a stitch you are unfamiliar with then we recommend practising first on a separate piece of material to perfect it before working on the hat. Unless otherwise stated, use a single thread that isn't longer than necessary to keep thread knotting to a minimum.

All of the stitches, with the exception of tie tacks, are started with a knot and fastened off by making a couple of tiny stitches on top of each other before snipping the thread. Always use an appropriate stitch length for your project. All stitches shown are for a right-handed sewer so adjust accordingly for left-handed sewing.

> **NOTE** Throughout the book, we have used contrasting thread in the step images to show the stitches clearly. For the actual projects, you should always use matching thread.

Knot

It all starts with a knot. A millinery knot secures the thread when starting to stitch instead of backstitching. We always avoid unnecessary stitches that could show on the right side of the hat. Keep knots small and as inconspicuous as possible.

To make a knot, wrap the end of the thread around your index finger. Roll and twist the thread off your finger using your thumb. Use the nail of your middle finger to pull the thread down, thus creating the knot.

Stab stitch

This stitch consists of tiny, practically invisible stitches on the right side of the fabric and a longer stitch inside. The inside stitch can vary in length depending on what you are sewing.

Work from right to left, starting with a knot on the wrong side of the fabric. Bring the needle through to the right side. Take the needle back to the wrong side just a fraction along and pull the thread taut. Make a longer stitch on the wrong side then push your needle back through to the right side to create the next stitch.

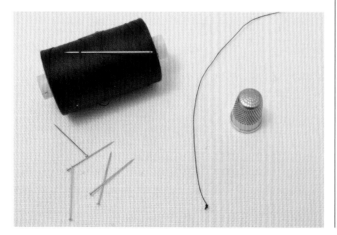

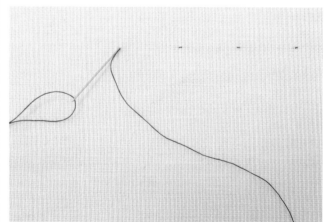

Diagonal stitch

This stitch can also be known as a slant stitch and is extremely versatile. It can be worked horizontally or vertically from left to right or right to left, depending on what is being worked.

Start with a knot on the wrong side of the fabric and then bring the needle through to the right side. Take the needle back through to the wrong side on a diagonal. Repeat until finished. On the reverse of the fabric your stitches will form straight lines.

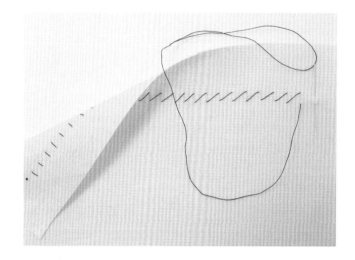

Tie tack

This stitch is ideal for securing veiling, intricate lace or other delicate fabrics. Tie tacks are made individually and spaced at intervals depending on what is being worked. They will be almost invisible when made in a thread that matches your work.

Leaving a long end of unknotted thread, take the needle through the material from the right side to the wrong side. Make a tiny stab stitch on the wrong side of the fabric and bring the needle back to the right side in the same place that you started. Snip the thread, ensuring there is enough to tie. Finish the stitch off by tying both ends together in a double knot before snipping close to the knot.

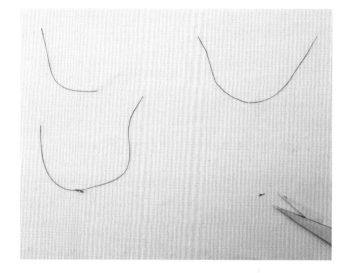

Slip stitch

As in dressmaking, this stitch is used to create a neat and smooth finish to a hem with no visible stitches.

Work this stitch from right to left. Take your knotted thread up into the fold of the turned edge to start. Slip the needle along the inside of the turned edge and then back out on the fold. Pick a tiny thread of the fabric just below the fold then take your needle back into the fold of the turned edge. Slip the needle along inside the fold to make your next stitch.

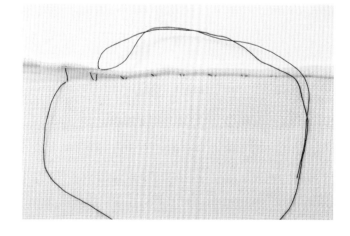

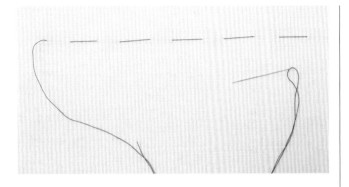

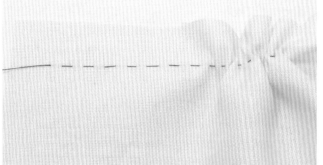

Tacking stitch

Also known in dressmaking as a basting stitch, this is a temporary stitch used to hold fabrics in place while the final stitching is being made. The needle is passed in and out of the material, making long stitches that are taken out afterwards.

Gathering or running stitch

This is used for any gathering, such as the ends of veiling or a gathered lining. It is a running stitch made from short, even stitches by passing the needle in and out of the fabric and securing at one end with a knot.

Whip stitch

Similar to an overcast stitch in dressmaking, this stitch is used for sewing two finished edges together when you want a neat and tidy finish. Tiny stitches appear on the wrong side of the join, and no stitches are visible on the right side.

1 Place the two edges together, exactly side by side with wrong sides facing. Work vertically from top to bottom, sewing towards yourself. Starting with a tiny knot, insert the needle in through one edge and pull through, hiding the knot in the seam. Pass the needle up and over both joins of material and insert back in as close to the first

stitch as you can. Continue in this way for the whole length of the seam, making tiny straight stitches across the join at equal distances very close together.

2 Pull each stitch firmly to draw the cut edges together and to sink the stitches into the material. When the seam is opened, the stitches you've done from the right side almost disappear into the seam.

3 The stitches are tiny and neat but visible from the wrong side.

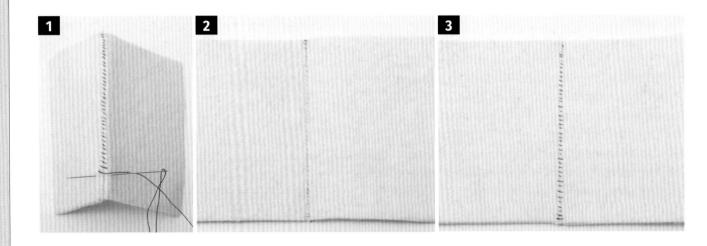

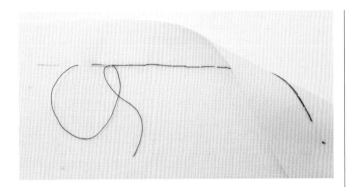

Backstitch

We most commonly use this stitch for sewing a crown to a brim. Work from right to left, starting with a knot on the wrong side of the fabric. Take the needle through to the right side, then insert back to the wrong side using an appropriate stitch length. Bring the needle back to the right side a full stitch's length ahead of the first stitch. Insert the needle back through to the wrong side at the point where the first stitch finished. Continue making the stitches in this way until the work is finished.

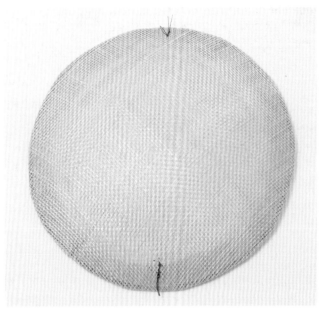

Front and back marks

These are temporary stitches used to mark the centre front and the centre back of your work. They are essential for achieving correct positioning when bringing a crown and brim together or when fitting and trimming. They are useful to leave in the work until the end. You can either mark the front with a cross and the back with a dash, or use different colour threads for dashes on both the front and back.

Blanket stitch

This is used for sewing the wire on the edge or in a fold of a brim or wherever else it is needed to shape a hat. It can also be called a wire stitch. It is essential that it is worked correctly to be efficient in holding the wire correctly.

Start with a knot and work the stitch from right to left. Pass the needle behind the edge of the brim and the wire. Pick up a small stitch just under the wire and pull the needle through but leave a loop. Pass the needle through this loop from the back. Pull it taut, holding the wire securely. Continue with approx. ¾in (2cm) between stitches. (See also Sewing in a Wire, pages 28–9.)

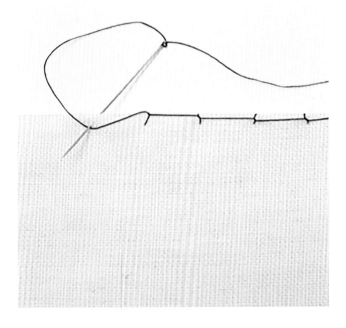

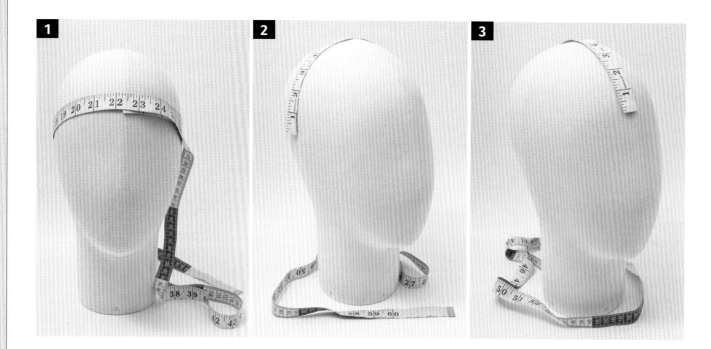

TAKING A HEAD MEASUREMENT

You can take the measurements for someone's head size in three easy steps. However, to accurately measure your own head size, you will need to get a friend involved, as it's difficult to see the measurements on your own.

1 Hold a dressmaker's tape around the head, in the middle of the forehead where you feel a hat sits most comfortably, and note the measurement. An average head size is around 22–22½in (56–57cm).

2 Take the measurement from side to side over the crown of the head to a place where the hat would sit comfortably.

3 Lastly, take the measurement from front to back, again over the crown of the head and in a place where a hat would sit comfortably. These measurements will be useful if you have to determine the correct depth of crown for a project.

TIP
As with everything in millinery, being precise with your measurements will ensure the best results.

BLOCKING

Central to good hat making is good blocking. Blocking is the name given to the process of moulding and manipulating flat pieces of material, or felt and straw hoods and capelines, onto blocks to form the shape of the hat.

We mostly use steam for blocking. This is done throughout the process as soon as the fabric starts to stiffen again. But sometimes a fine spray of water is helpful to soften materials to work on, securing materials to the block with pins and blocking cord. When dry they retain the shape of the block that they were worked on.

Professional hat steamers are available to buy, but they are expensive and unnecessary for the home milliner who can obtain all the steam required with an ordinary household kettle. You will need to keep the lid of the kettle open while steaming to prevent it from switching off. Don't fill the kettle too full otherwise it may bubble and spit out droplets of boiling water, but pay attention to the water level at all times to avoid the kettle boiling dry. Steam will burn you so always hold your work well above the kettle opening where the steam is softer.

TIP

Always start by covering the block with food wrap or a clean plastic bag. This is to prevent materials from sticking to the block and to avoid any marks from the block transferring to your work. Secure underneath the block with sticky tape.

Bottom left *A parasisal straw cone blocked on a pillbox-shaped hat block, showing the use of pins to secure at the pin line.*

Below *A velour felt capeline blocked on a dome-shaped hat block, showing pins and use of a blocking cord to secure while drying.*

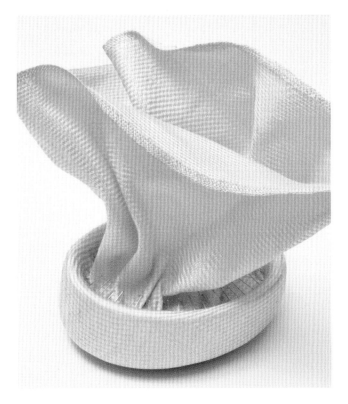

Blocking a sinamay crown

1 Cut a square of sinamay that is large enough for your crown block. With the points of the square to the front, back and sides (the bias), pull the sinamay over the block and roughly secure with a few pins and a blocking cord.

2 Arrange the sinamay on the block a little more by evenly pinning the four corners of the square (the bias) at the front, the back and at both sides. The straights of the fabric will lie in between the four points of bias. Pin these four straights well, as there will be no more movement of the fabric on the straight. Work the excess fabric towards the bias points, pushing the cord down towards its finishing point, and re-tightening as necessary with a pin as you work. The aim is to get as smooth a finish with as few gathers as possible.

3 Different fabrics will have different amounts of 'give' on the bias. Sinamay becomes very flexible when steamed but, depending on the depth of crown being blocked, you may have unavoidable gathers at all four points of bias. These gathers will need to be disguised by the trimming. You will be able to pull most of the excess fullness out by working sections at a time. Hold the area to be worked under the steam until you can feel the fabric become soft and pliable. When it is soft and pliable, pull, pin in place and re-tighten the blocking cord.

4 Most pre-stiffened sinamays will hold their shape well but we would recommend using at least two layers of pre-stiffened sinamay for a crown. Depending on the quality of the sinamay and the design of the finished hat you may need three layers, but only experience and trial and error will let you know.

Repeat Steps 1–3 to block another layer or two on top of the first one. You will not need to let each individual layer dry before working another one on top, but when finished the whole blocked crown must be left to dry fully before removing from the block. Always make a front and a back mark (see page 21 for information) before removing any work from the block.

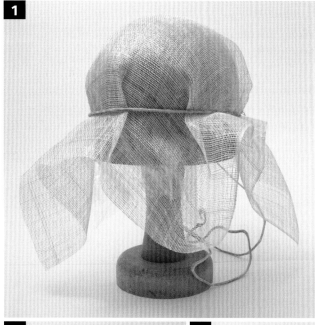

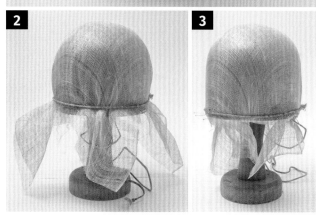

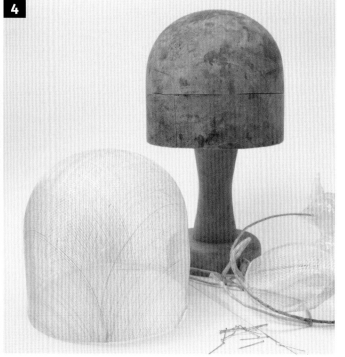

Blocking buckram

Buckram behaves in a similar way to sinamay in as much as when held under the steam it becomes soft and pliable. This means you will be able to block a buckram crown in the same way as a sinamay one. However, it does not have quite as much 'give' on the bias and you won't be able to achieve the same depth of crown as with sinamay. Buckram is very suitable for brims, shallow crown shapes and headpieces such as the Bridal Headdress on page 136.

TIP

If you have a lot of steaming to do make sure you are in a well-ventilated room to avoid steaming up – you need to be able to see what you are doing!

Blocking straws and felts

Straws and felts are generally supplied as hoods or capelines. Hoods are only suitable for crowns or hats with very small brims, such as trilbys or cloches, whereas capelines are suitable for larger brimmed hats. However, different suppliers sell different sized hoods and capelines, so you will need to check before deciding on the size of felt or straw you need to buy for any particular project.

Felt will need to be held in the steam until it is damp and hot before it becomes pliable enough to work with. Straws require a slightly different approach, as they don't need as much steam and are often very responsive to blocking after being sprayed with water. Neither felts nor straws have bias and straights like flat fabrics, but both are blocked in the same way: working on sections at a time, steaming or spraying with water, then pulling, pinning and securing with a blocking cord.

Straw hoods and capelines are a woven material and sometimes have a square or a diamond shape at the very centre of the hood or capeline where the weave has started. It is important when blocking a crown that this shape in the straw is central to the block; if it isn't, the finished piece of blocking can appear lopsided.

When working with felt or straw hoods or capelines, we would always recommend blocking the brim before blocking the crown. If there isn't quite enough material after blocking the brim the crown can always be made deeper by adding a bias strip of buckram to the bottom edge that can be covered by the trim. You cannot add to a brim quite so easily.

It is the same process for blocking brims as it is for crowns. The material being used is fixed roughly in place using pins and a blocking cord before being arranged some more, then worked in sections using steam until all excess material has been pulled out and the material lies smooth and snug against the block being worked on.

WORKING WITH WIRE

Millinery wire is sold in coils and one of the most important aspects of working with wire is removing the spring and the twist before working with it. You do not need to take out all the curve in the wire – this can be shaped and manipulated while sewing into your project. But if you don't deal with the spring your project will take on the same shape as the wire.

We generally use a US 16 gauge (SWG 18, 1.25mm) wire when making hats and often use a US 26 gauge (SWG 27, 0.4mm) wire for trims, which is very soft and doesn't have the same kind of spring in it. This can usually be worked into your projects without the attention the harder wire needs.

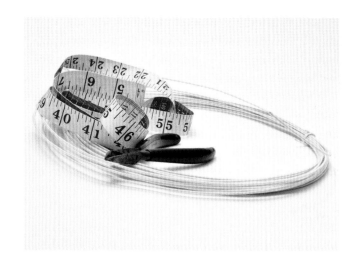

1

2

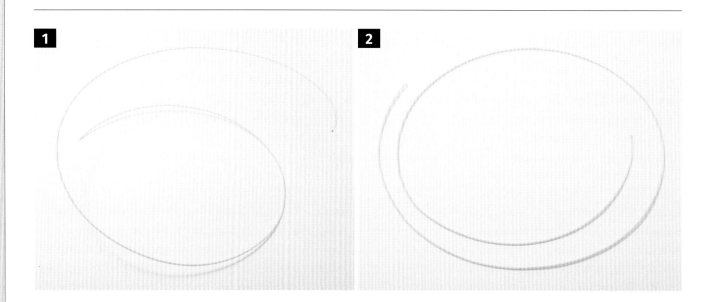

Removing the spring and twist from wire

1 Cut the required amount of wire using wire cutters or pliers with a cutting edge.

2 Take the spring out by manipulating it with your fingers until it lays flat on a surface such as a table.

TIP

The use of wire in millinery is very important and it's well worth taking a little time getting used to the handling of it. Too much wire, or too little, or not taking out the spring effectively could throw the shape out completely. Be patient with wire!

Joining a wire shape

The style of hat or headpiece and the fabric that it is being made in will often inform your choices of techniques to use, as will experience. Joining the wire before sewing it into the work is a technique that we have chosen to use in some of the projects.

1 Cut the required amount of wire (ensuring there will be enough for an appropriate overlap) using wire cutters or pliers with a cutting edge then remove the twist and spring from the wire (see opposite).

2 Join the two ends of wire together at the centre of the overlap by making a simple hitch knot. Make a loop with a double thread then pass the two ends of thread through that loop.

3 Wrap the thread tightly around the wire, working towards one end. When you reach the end, wrap the thread tightly over the two pieces of wire, securing well before working back towards the other end in a criss-cross pattern.

4 When you reach the other end, wrap the thread tightly over the two wires, securing well before working back to the centre of the join.

5 Wrap the thread over the wire at the centre of the join several times before finishing off by making a loop and passing the ends through as in step 2.

6 Trim off any ends of thread.

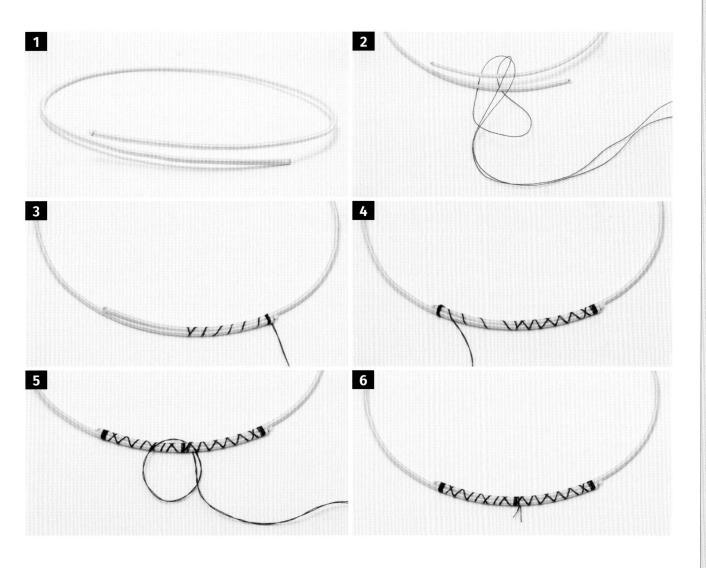

Sewing wire into a folded edge

A wire goes in a folded edge when there is a seam allowance to be turned or rolled over to hide the wire.

1 Cut the required amount of wire for your project, ensuring there is enough for an overlapped join. The length of the join in the wire will depend on the size of the project and will become obvious with experience. Remove the spring and the twist from the wire (see page 26). Start the wire beyond the back mark – exactly where will depend on the length of join; you want to aim for the centre of the join being at the centre back mark of your project. Make a couple of stab stitches (see page 18) on top of each other to secure.

2 Use a blanket stitch (see page 21).

3 Make a tiny stitch on the right side of the fabric. When you are working with a thread that matches the colour of your fabric this tiny stitch won't be seen.

4 Bring your needle back through to the wrong side of the fabric on the other side of the wire, then through the loop of thread.

5 Pull the thread to make the stitch nice and tight against the wire before making your next stitch. Continue in this way all around the edge.

6 Finish the wire beyond the back mark so there is an equal amount of double wire either side of the back mark. Join the two ends of wire together by using blanket stitch over both wires. Oversew the two ends of wire a couple of times to ensure the wires are firmly stitched together.

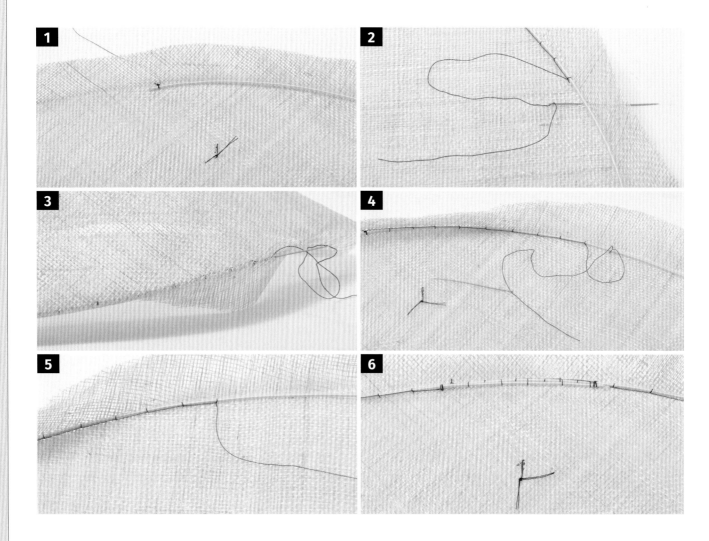

Sewing wire onto a cut edge

A wire goes in a cut edge when a separate bind is used for finishing an edge, either to cover it or when it gets covered by the material that the hat is made in. The purpose of wire is to keep the shape and form of the hat, so it is purely functional. Binds on hats can be decorative if using a contrasting fabric.

Sewing a wire into a project that has a cut edge is a very similar process and uses the same stitch as when sewing one into a folded edge. Because you are working on the edge of the fabric you do not need to make the tiny stab stitch through to the right side of the fabric.

1 Cut the required amount of wire for your project, ensuring there is enough for an overlapped join. The length of the join in the wire will depend on the size of the project and will become obvious with experience. Remove the spring and the twist from the wire (see page 26). Start the wire beyond the back mark – exactly where will depend on the length of join; you want to aim for the centre of the join being at the centre back mark of your project. Working just inside the edge of the wrong side of the material, make a couple of stab stitches on top of each other to secure.

2 Use a blanket stitch (see page 21). Bring your needle through from the right side to the wrong side and under the loop of thread.

3 Pull the thread to make the stitch nice and tight against the wire before making your next stitch. Continue in this way all around the edge.

4 Finish the wire beyond the back mark so there is an equal amount of double wire either side of the back mark. Join the two ends of wire together by using blanket stitch over both wires. Oversew the two ends of wire a couple of times to ensure they are firmly stitched together.

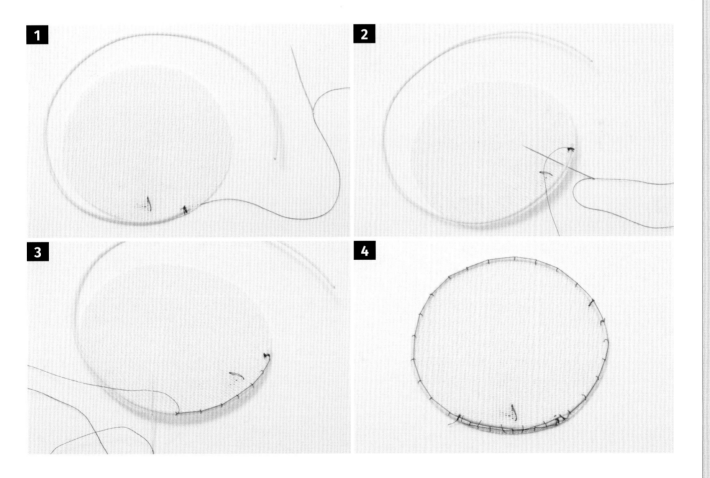

SEWING IN A PETERSHAM RIBBON

Petersham ribbon is used to create the correct head fitting by cutting a length the same size as the head fitting needed and adding a little extra for the seam allowance then easing and sewing it into the hat where it fits the head. If it is a smaller-shaped hat that fits just over the crown of the head, then a petersham ribbon is sewn in to give a nice finish and grips can be used between stitches to grip onto the hair. A comb or Alice band can also be sewn onto the petersham. We use either a no. 5 or a no. 3 size petersham for all our hats.

1 Measure the head fitting you want your hat size to be (see page 22). We are using the average head size, which is 22½in (57cm). Measure in ¾in (2cm) from one end of the petersham and put a pin in. From this pin measure 22½in (57cm) along and mark with another pin. Cut the petersham off another ¾in (2cm) away from the pin.

2 Pin your first pin in the petersham onto the centre back of the head fitting line inside the hat. Now fold over the other end of petersham where the pin mark is and pin this directly on top of the centre back where your first pin is.

3 Now pin the petersham onto the centre front mark with equal measurements of petersham either side.

4 Steadily work your way round both sides, easing the petersham in and evenly placing pins roughly 1in (2.5cm) apart. Make sure you are following a nice straight even line where the head fitting is.

5 Knot a single thread at one end in a colour to match the petersham and hat (we are using black thread here to show up in photographs). Don't have the thread too long as it will keep knotting up but make sure it is long enough to sew around the petersham. Push the needle in, coming from the right side of the hat so it comes out on the top edge of the folded petersham at the centre back.

6 Place the needle back in directly into the hat just above the petersham edge where the thread is coming out and pull the thread taut. This is your first tiny stitch.

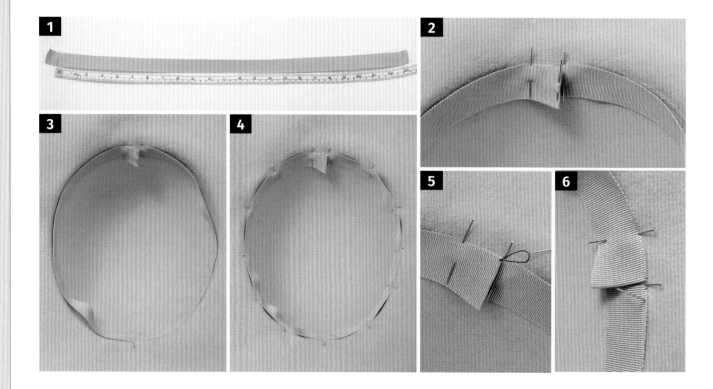

7 Move along approx. ⅛in (3mm) to the right and have your needle come out on the petersham edge and go back in directly into the hat just above the petersham edge as before. Pull the thread taut. Carry on like this all the way around until you get to the centre back. Your stitches will look like this and hardly be seen when the thread colour is matching.

8 This is what your stitches will look like from the right side of the hat.

9 To finish off the centre back, do three tiny stab stitches (see page 18) to join the petersham edges together.

10 This is what your finished petersham should look like!

11 If your petersham is for a smaller shape with a curved edge, it helps to first curve the petersham with an iron. This will make the petersham easier to fit into the shape. On an ironing board, using your fingers, curve the petersham in one hand and iron as you go along.

12 To fit petersham into a corner of a shape, fold one side over the other.

13 To make the join in a petersham on a corner, have a folded end on top of a flat end.

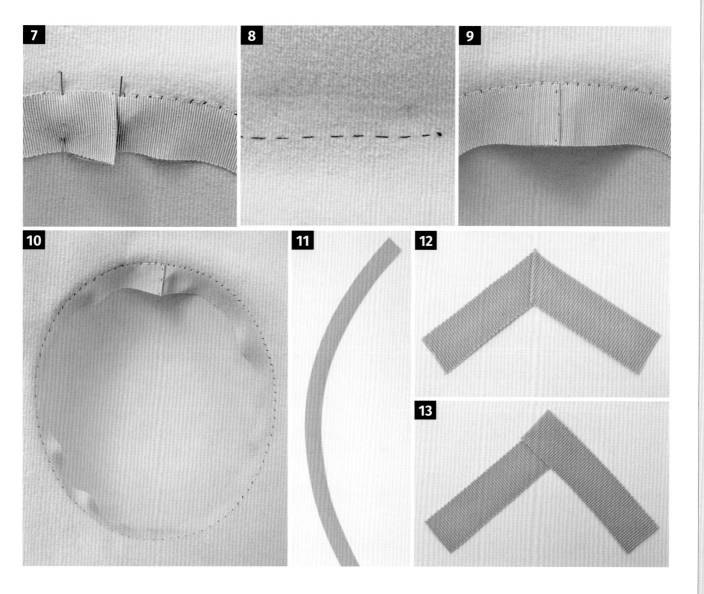

LININGS

Linings are used to neaten up the appearance of the inside of a hat, for comfort, and to cover any stitches that may be showing. The lining can be in a shade to complement the hat colour or a complete contrast for something more striking.

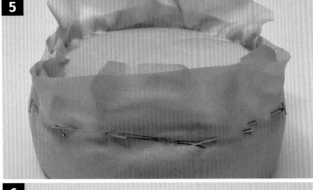

Tip and side band lining

This lining can be made using a sewing machine or sewn by hand and on the same block as the crown of the hat. The instructions that follow are for making the tip and side band lining for the project on page 106 but one for any shape of crown block can be made in the same way.

1 To determine the amount of fabric you need for your lining, first measure the circumference of your block. Add 1in (2.5cm) for the seam allowance.

2 Measure the depth of the side band from the tip edge to the finish of the block. For this lining we measure to the underside of the block's pin line. Add 1in (2.5cm) for the seam allowance. Cut a bias strip of lining to your required measurements.

3 Using a little tension, pull the bias strip of lining fabric around the side band of the block, right side down, so that it fits snugly. Pin a back seam and remove from the block.

4 Sew the back seam on a sewing machine, or sew by hand using a backstitch (see page 21). Trim back the seam allowance to ⅜in (1cm). Press the seam open and put the stitched side band back on to the block, pinning to secure.

5 Cut a 9in (23cm) square of lining and place right side down onto the tip of the block with the bias to the front. Pin where the tip meets the side band in four places: the front, back and at both sides. Fill in the rest with a row of pins along the same line. Sew a tacking line (see page 20) around the line of pins then take the pins out. Wave the lining in the steam for a few seconds and allow to dry. Take the lining off the block and sew by machine or by hand using a backstitch.

6 Put the lining back on the block, using pins to secure it at the pin line. Cut the seam allowance back to ⅜in (1cm) and press open. Wave the lining in the steam for a few seconds to set it. Leave to dry. Only take it off the block when you are ready to use it so it keeps its pressed shape.

Making a gathered lining

Gathered linings are normally only seen in handmade hats due to the hand sewing involved. They are simple to make and give a beautiful, luxurious finish. No block is needed to make them; they are made from a flat piece of fabric. They can be used when the crown isn't too tight fitting, as you need a small amount of space for the gathers between the top of the head and the tip of the crown.

1 Cut a bias strip of any lightweight fabric 23½ x 9in (60 x 23cm) wide. With right sides facing fold the length in half, pin then sew a back seam using a ½in (1cm) seam allowance. We have machine stitched our seam but as it's not a long seam and doesn't need to be very strong, stitching by hand using a backstitch would be fine.

2 Working on the wrong side of the fabric, press the back seam to one side and make a ½in (1.5cm) turning at the top.

3 Run a line of gathering stitches (see page 20) mid way through this top turning.

These are instructions for making a gathered lining for a hat with a head fitting of 22½in (57cm) and a crown depth of 8in (20cm). You can adjust these measurements and make a gathered lining for any size of hat by measuring its inside circumference around the head fitting, and the depth of crown from the centre point to the head fitting and adding a seam allowance.

4 Draw up the gathering stitches.

5 When you are left with a small circle, finish off the thread by securing well with a couple of tiny stab stitches (see page 18) on top of each other.

6 On the wrong side, pin a small piece of the same lining fabric to cover the circle.

7 Stitch in place.

COVERING A METAL ALICE BAND

Our preferred method of attaching a small hat or headpiece securely to the head is by fixing it to a metal Alice band. There are a couple of advantages to covering your metal Alice band before fixing to your hat. Firstly, because embroidery thread is available in such a huge range of colours, you can choose a colour to match your hair colour so the Alice band 'disappears' when wearing, or you can choose a contrasting colour to make it a feature. And secondly, covering the Alice band will enable a firmer fix when stitching it to the piece, as you can catch some of the covering thread with each fixing stitch.

1 Place a small amount of all-purpose glue on the underside of one end of the Alice band and stick on the end of a skein of embroidery thread, so that it is facing towards the centre of the band.

2 Wrap the thread over the stuck end, working towards the centre of the band.

3 Cover the metal completely by continuing to wrap the thread until you reach the centre. Cut the thread and stick with a small amount of glue.

4 Repeat the process from the other end, tidily finishing off at the centre with a small amount of glue.

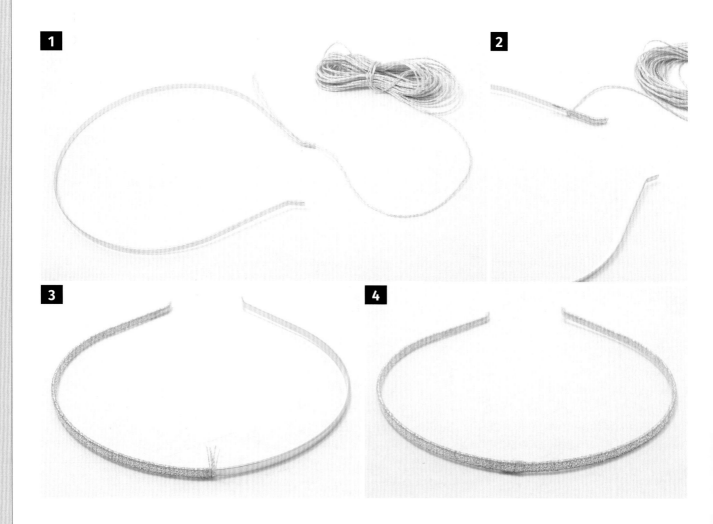

SEWING IN A COVERED ALICE BAND

The Alice band can be stitched to petersham ribbon or, depending on the style and trim of your work, stitched all the way through to the right side. If it is being stitched all the way through to the right side you will get a good fix, but be aware that your stitches will show.

Sew the band to both the right and the left side of the work by oversewing it several times, catching the embroidery thread with each stitch. Use a short, strong, double thread, finishing it off securely when the band is firmly in place.

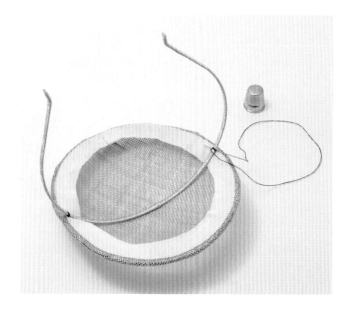

"When love and skill work together, expect a masterpiece."

JOHN RUSKIN
Art critic

HOW TO USE THE PATTERNS

You will need to transfer the patterns onto sheets of paper. You can either use a photocopier, or transfer them by hand using the grid as a guide. Each square on the grid measures ³⁄₁₆in (0.5cm). If, for example, you need to copy a pattern at 200%, you would draw a grid with squares measuring double the original size, i.e. ³⁄₈in (1cm).

Once you have transferred the patterns, it is important to be accurate when cutting them out. Adding or taking away even the smallest amount by mistake can alter the shape dramatically.

Throughout the patterns we have indicated the centre front by using a dash and the centre back with a dot. The arrows on all pattern pieces indicate the line of bias.

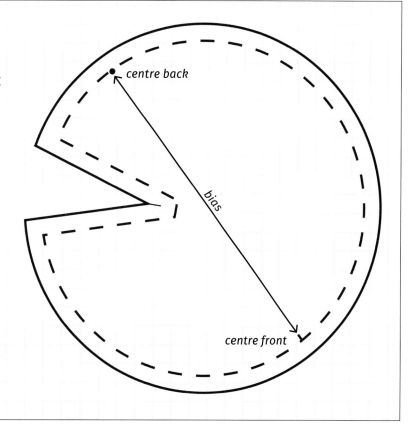

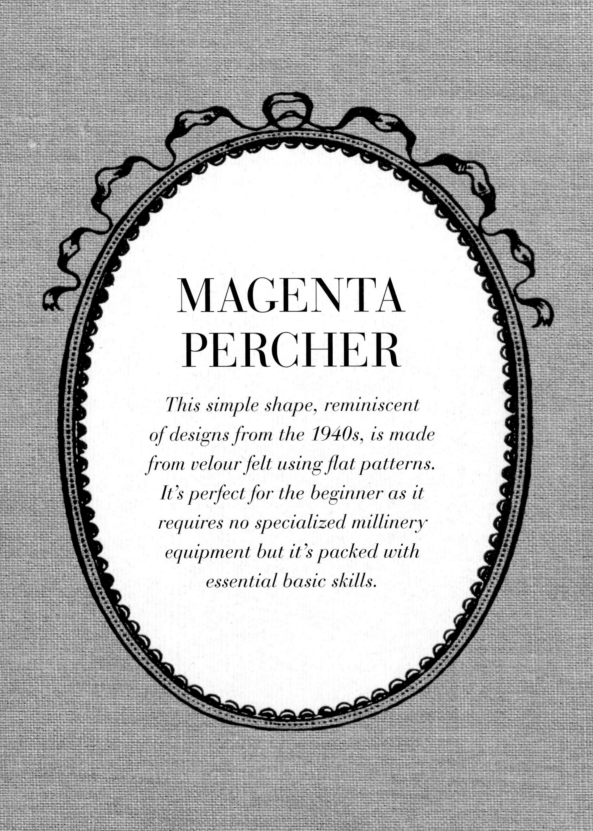

MAGENTA PERCHER

This simple shape, reminiscent of designs from the 1940s, is made from velour felt using flat patterns. It's perfect for the beginner as it requires no specialized millinery equipment but it's packed with essential basic skills.

You will need:

The base and brim patterns
Pliers with a cutting edge
Needles
Sewing thread in colours to match
    chosen fabrics
Thimble
Pins
Tape measure
Scissors
Iron
Felt-tip pen
Pencil
All-purpose glue

For the base and brim:
22in (56cm) length of US 16 gauge
    (SWG 18, 1.2mm) millinery wire
Magenta velour felt cone
Alice band and embroidery thread
    to cover

For the trim:
A collection of feathers including
    two arrowhead quills and some
    stripped coque

Making the base

1 Take out any spring or twist in the wire (see page 26) and shape it to the base pattern. Transfer the front and back marks from the pattern to the wire using a pencil.

2 Join the ends of the wire with a 2in (5cm) overlap (see page 27).

3 Shape the wire to fit your own head. Gently curve the wire over the crown of the head.

4 Place the wire on the wrong side of the felt cone along its bottom edge and pin across the wire. Cut around the wire leaving approx. 1in (2.5cm) allowance for turnings.

5 Sew the wire to the felt using the technique for sewing wire into a folded edge on page 28. On the right side of the felt, put your needle back as close as possible to the same hole it came out of so the stitch isn't visible on the right side.

6 Using a felt-tip pen, mark ⅜in (1cm) from the edge of the wire all around the shape and trim back to the marks.

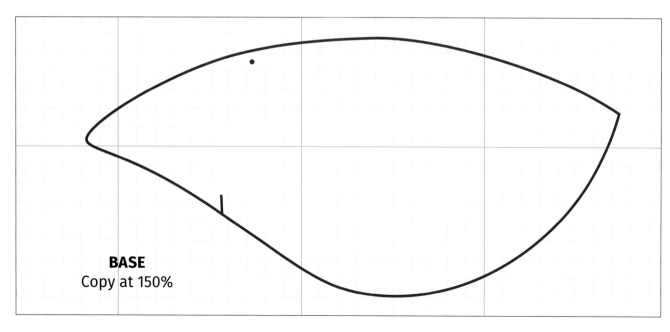

BASE
Copy at 150%

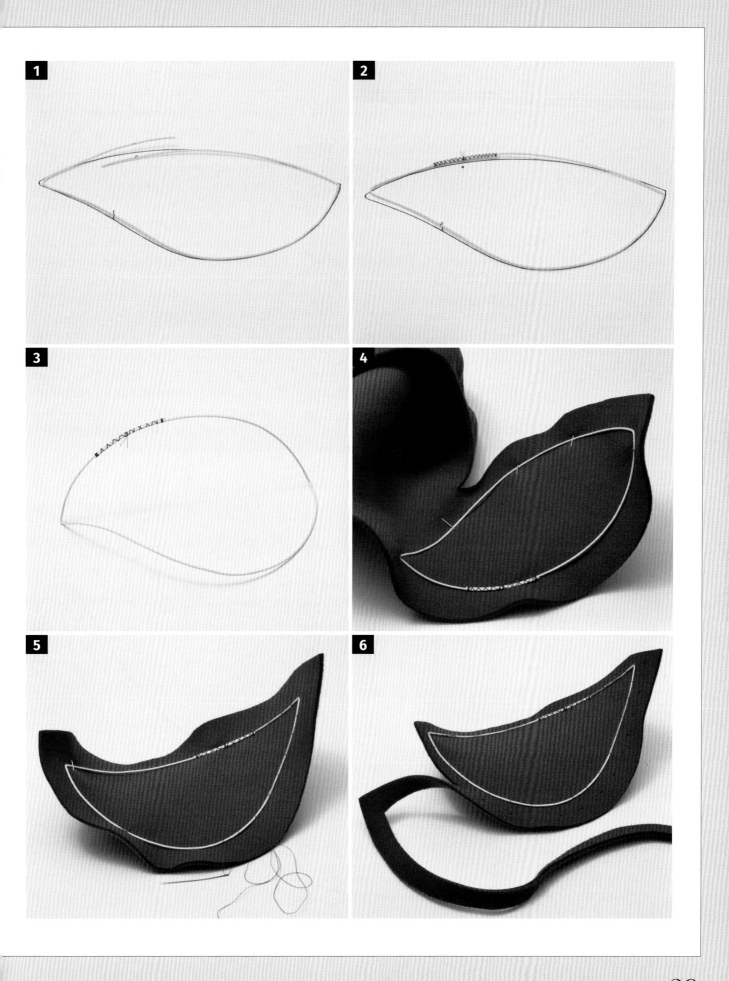

7 Stitch the turning back using small stab stitches (see page 18), going all the way through to the right side of the felt.

8 On the right side of the felt, put your needle back as close as possible to the same hole it came out of so the stitch isn't visible on the right side (see step 5).

9 At both points of the piece, you will need to create a mitred join. Bring both turnings together at each point to determine how much felt you need to cut out.

10 Both points are a different shape so you will need to cut out a different amount of felt at either end, as shown. Use whip stitch to join the two edges of cut felt (see page 20).

11 Stitch a front and back mark using the base pattern (see page 38) as a guide. Use different colour threads so you know which is front and which is back. We've used black for the back and white for the front.

Making the brim

12 Transfer the brim pattern (below) onto paper. Cut the pattern out and pin onto the remainder of the velour cone.

13 Cut out the brim and transfer the front and back marks with a stitch (see step 11).

14 Working on the wrong side of the felt, bring together the two edges of the cut-out 'V' and join together using whip stitch (see page 20).

15 Pin the brim to the base ⅜in (1cm) in from the edge of the base. Match the front and back marks of the brim to the ones on the base. When the front of the piece is facing you, the whipped 'V' of the brim will meet the right-hand point of the base and the left-hand side of the brim will meet the left-hand point of the base.

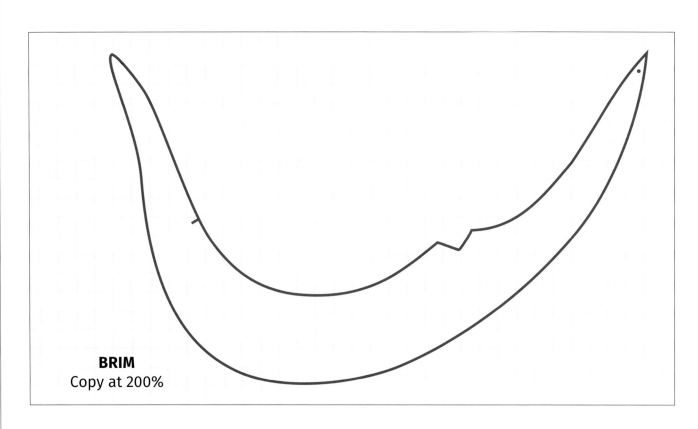

BRIM
Copy at 200%

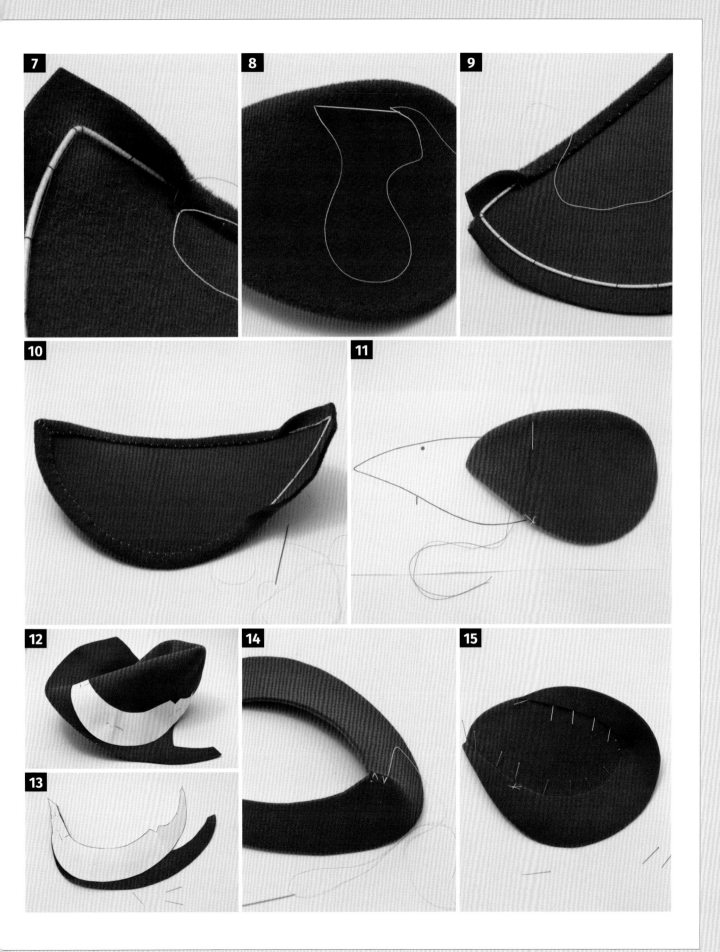

16 Stitch the brim to the base using a small stab stitch (see page 18) going all the way through to the wrong side of the piece.

17 Try to keep your stitches invisible on the inside by putting your needle back as close as possible to the same hole it came out of.

Attaching the Alice band
18 Cover an Alice band with embroidery thread (see page 34). Mark with a pin 1¼in (3cm) from the bottom of the band on one side and 5in (12.5cm) on the other.

19 Sew the Alice band onto the base (see page 35). With the front of the piece facing you the pin marking 1¼in (3cm) is sewn onto the point of the left-hand side and the pin marking 5in (12.5cm) is sewn onto the point of the right-hand side.

Adding the trimming
20 Choose a selection of feathers for the trimming, including a couple of arrowhead quills for some height and structure. We haven't wanted to be too prescriptive with the trim as this percher will suit a variety of different feathers and arrangements.

21 Bunch the feathers that you are using into a pleasing selection and shape and securely sew to the base using a stab stitch through the quills and stems. Tiny feathers can be added to the arrangement using all-purpose glue.

22 You've finished!

TIP
When the piece is finished, hold a clothes brush in the steam from a kettle for a few seconds then use it to lift the pile of the felt.

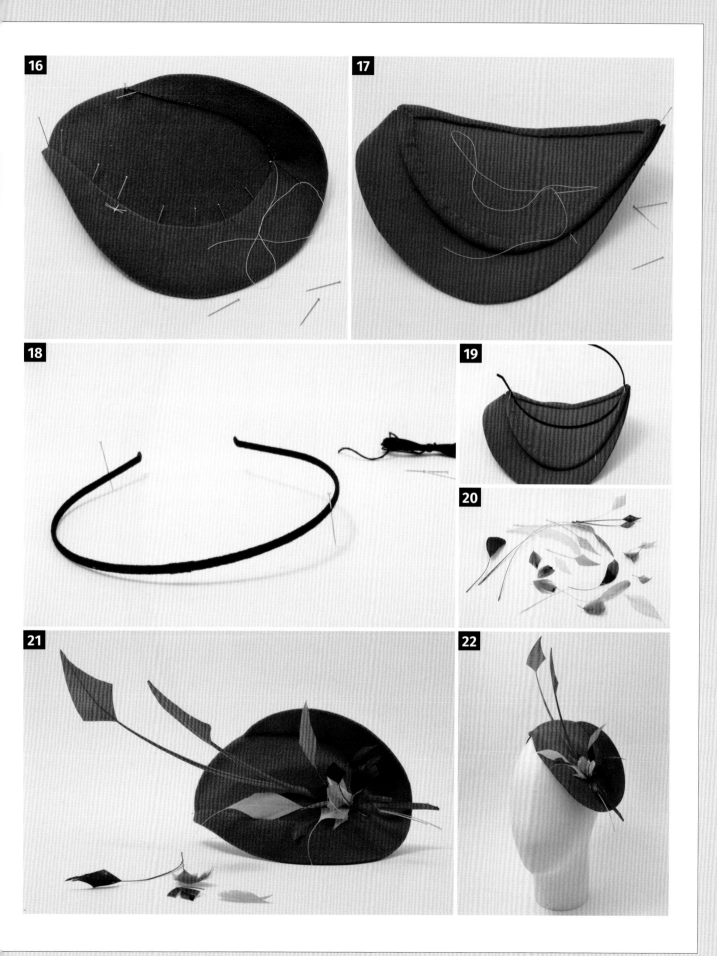

FELT CAPELINE

*This modern, wearable hat is a
simple beginner's project requiring
only a standard dome hat block.
Made from a luxurious velour felt,
it can be worn with jeans and any
style of jacket for some instant
winter style and glamour.*

You will need:

Dome block
Food wrap
Sticky tape
Kettle or hat steamer
Blocking cord
Pins (blocking and dressmaking)
Needles
Sewing thread in colours to match
    chosen fabrics
Thimble
Iron and ironing board
Cotton pressing cloth
Small bowl of water
Scissors
Felt-tip pen
Small piece of medium-grade sandpaper
Tape measure
Bradawl or point of sharp scissors
All-purpose glue

For the hat:
Single-sided velour felt capeline
23½in (59.5cm) of no. 5 petersham
    ribbon for head fitting in colour
    to match felt

For the belt:
30½in (77.5cm) mock snakeskin trim
Thread in felt colour
Buckle to fit width of snakeskin
Eyelet kit

TIP

Running sandpaper along the brim edge softens any scissor marks where you've cut the felt, to achieve a nice smooth line.

Shaping the hat

1 Cover your dome block with food wrap and secure underneath with sticky tape (see page 23). Steam the crown of the velour capeline until it's soft and damp. Pull it gently over the dome so that it sits snug and smooth against the block. Secure with a blocking cord and pins at the point where the capeline flares out to the brim (see page 25). Leave to dry.

2 When it's dry, sew a front and back mark. Gently take it off the block. Sew in a no.5 petersham ribbon to fit the head fitting inside (see page 30).

3 Place the capeline on a flat surface – an ironing board is ideal. Wet a piece of cotton pressing cloth in a small bowl of water, then using a steam iron press the brim flat. Wet the cloth between each pressing as this prevents the velour from crushing. A lot of steam will be created while pressing. Work your way around the brim, being careful not to flatten where the crown joins the brim – try to keep the gentle curve there.

4 On the top side of the brim, measure from the head fit (the petersham ribbon sewing line) out to the edge of brim at equal intervals to make the brim the same width all the way around. Mark with a tacking line (see page 20) and trim off any excess with large, smooth cutting strokes to keep the edge nice and curved with no jagged bits.

5 Carefully rub some sandpaper along the edge to give the brim a softer look.

6 From the centre front mark, measure and pin 3in (7.5cm) to the right. This is to mark the positioning where the buckle will sit.

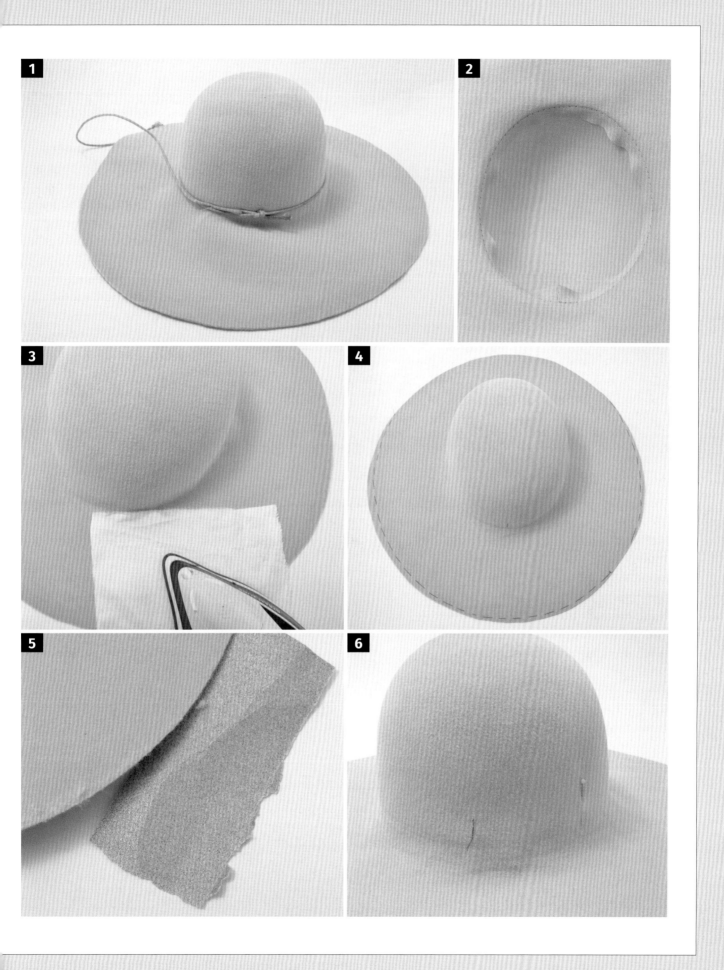

10 Working on the wrong side, trim off the triangle leaving ¼in (0.6cm) seam allowance. With a dab of glue, fold down firmly.

11 Approx. ¾in (2cm) in from the other end of snakeskin, using a bradawl or the point of sharp scissors, pierce the snakeskin in the centre. Slip the buckle on and push the prong through then secure the end on the wrong side with some tiny stab stitches (see page 18).

12 To make the belt loop, take a piece of mock snakeskin and cut a length approx. 2¼in (5.5cm) long. Trim the width to ¾in (2cm) and fold over ¼in (0.6cm) onto the back on both sides and glue down to make a finished width of ⅜in (1cm).

13 Place the loop around the belt strap and sew the ends of the loop together at the back with little stab stitches then fasten the buckle, pushing the strap through the loop.

Attaching the belt and adjusting the brim

14 Put the snakeskin belt onto the crown so that it fits nicely around the head fitting, covering the petersham stitches, and the buckle placement is on top of the pin mark.

15 Lift the petersham band inside the hat out of the way to sew some tiny stab stitches approx. 2in (5cm) apart around the belt to keep it in place. Your stitches on the inside will be covered by the petersham band.

16 Holding the front of brim, lightly steam to soften the edge and create a gentle curving shape. You've finished!

Making the belt

7 Measure and cut approx. 28in (71cm) of mock snakeskin trimming. To work out the eyelet position that will go through the buckle, measure approx. 3½in (9cm) from one end. Mark the position on the back of the trimming in the centre of band with a felt-tip pen.

8 Follow the instructions on the eyelet packet to make an eyelet. Then make two more eyelets approx. ¾in (2cm) to the right from the first eyelet with ¾in (2cm) between them.

9 Working on the wrong side of the mock snakeskin, fold the end of the belt up to the top edge to form a triangle approx. 1in (2.5cm) from the last eyelet.

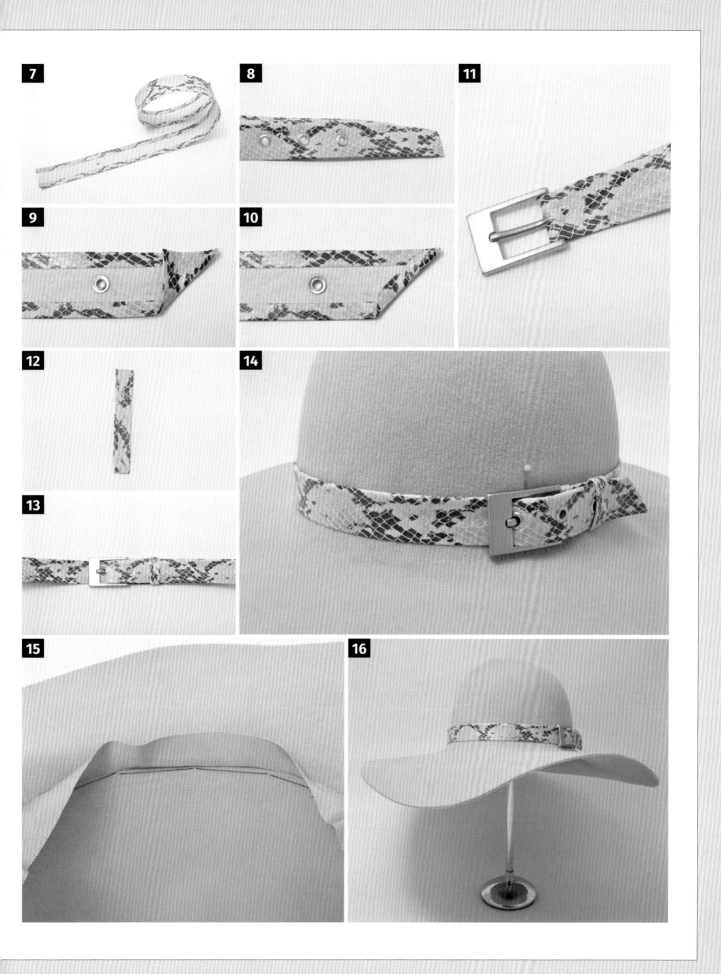

EVENING COCKTAIL BAND

Although we've called this an evening cocktail band, it is also more than suitable for any daytime event that needs a little bit of sparkle. Made with a flat pattern, this is another ideal starter project for aspiring milliners.

You will need:

The pattern for the headband
Pliers with a cutting edge
Pins
Needles
Thimble
Sewing thread in colours to match
    chosen fabrics
Tape measure
Scissors
Pencil
Iron
All-purpose glue

For the band:
11 x 3in (28 x 7.5cm) bias strip
    of buckram
24½in (62cm) length of US 16 gauge
    (SWG18, 1.2mm) millinery wire
23 x 1in (58.5 x 2.5cm) bias strip
    of tarlatan
11 x 3in (28 x 7.5cm) bias strip
    of black satin
11 x 3in (28 x 7.5cm) bias strip
    of silk or any other lightweight
    fabric for the lining
11 x 3in (28 x 7.5cm) bias strip
    of fusible interlining

For the veil and comb:
21 x at least 9in (53.5 x 23cm)
    veiling (if the veiling is wider
    it can be cut back)
1 metal comb

Making the band

1 Transfer the headband pattern on page 54 to a piece of paper (see page 35), marking the front and back marks (see page 21). Cut the pattern out and draw around it on to the strip of buckram. Cut out the shape and transfer front and back marks with a pencil.

2 Shape the length of millinery wire to the pattern. Using the pattern for reference, transfer the front and back marks to the wire with a pencil.

3 Sew the wire to the buckram (see page 29). The front and back marks on the wire should match with those on the buckram and you should have an approx. 2in (5cm) overlap of wire.

4 Gently bend the wire and shape the buckram to fit your head.

5 Gently pull the strip of tarlatan to help it lie flat when you sew it on and fold in half lengthways. Cut the strip back to approx. ¼in (0.6cm) wide.

6 Place the folded tarlatan over the edge of the buckram piece. Using a stab stitch (see page 18), sew the tarlatan to the edge of the band, covering the wire.

7 Use your fingers and a small amount of water to slightly dampen the tarlatan edge and press with the tip of the iron to flatten and smooth.

8 Pin the strip of black satin to the buckram band, gently pulling on the bias as you pin to help the fabric lie flat.

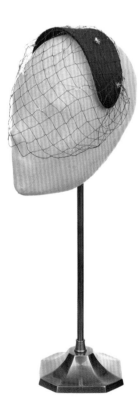

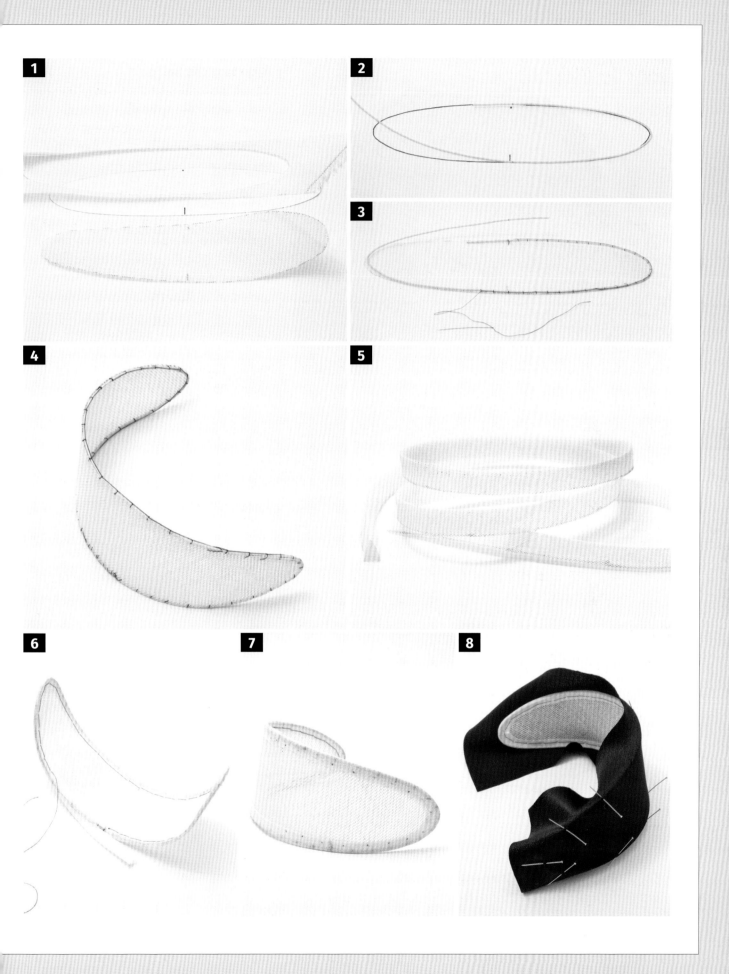

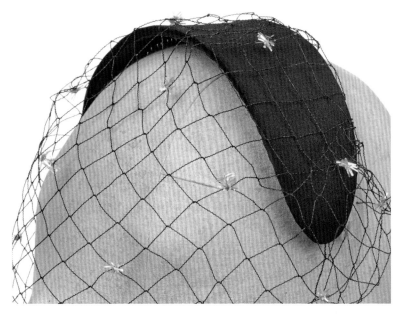

Attaching the lining

12 Iron the fusible interlining to the lining fabric. On the wrong side of the fabric, draw around the headband pattern with a pencil and cut out ¼in (0.6cm) larger than the pattern.

13 Pin the lining to the inside of the band, ensuring what will be the turning is equidistant from the edge of the band all the way around.

14 Stick the lining to the inside of the band, leaving ½in (1.5cm) from the wire edge free of glue. Use the glue sparingly to ensure none comes through to the right side.

15 Turn under the excess lining material all around the edge of the band. Pin the lining in place and using tiny slip stitches (see page 19), sew it to the turned-over edge.

16 Sew a centre back mark onto the centre of the back edge of the band.

9 Keeping the pins in place, trim back the satin to ½in (1.5cm) from the edge of the band all the way around the piece.

10 Snip into this turned-over edge every ½in (1.5cm), taking care not to snip too close to the edge of the band.

11 Glue the turned-over edge to the inside of the band. Use the glue sparingly so that none comes through and marks the right side of the material.

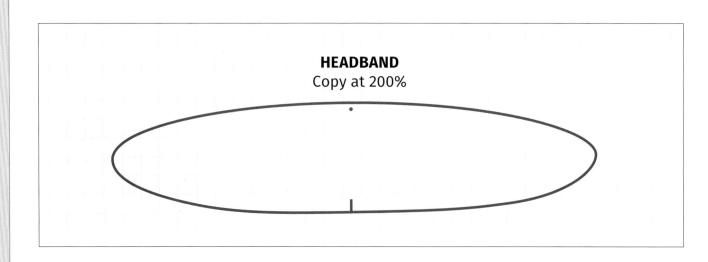

HEADBAND
Copy at 200%

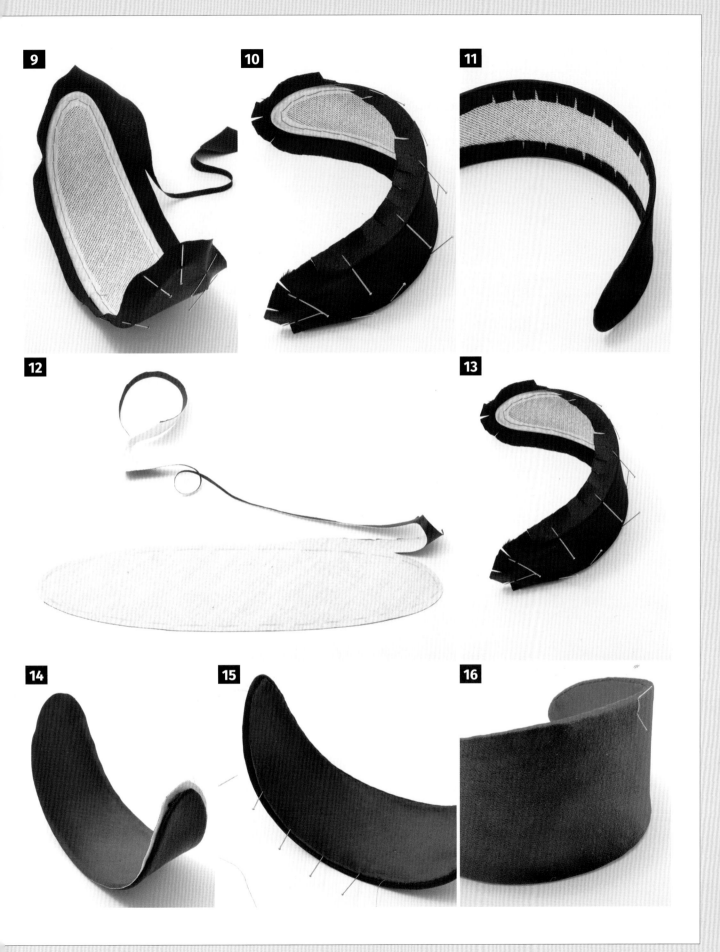

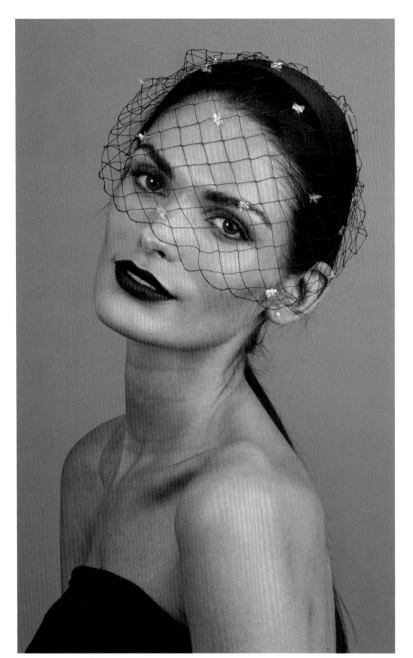

Making the veil

17 Gather up both sides of the veiling with a running stitch (see page 20).

18 Find the centre of your veiling and pin this onto the centre back mark of the band. Distribute the veiling equally down to both ends of the band. Pin along the edge using fine pins so as not to mark the satin. If there is an excess length of veiling, trim off.

19 Using tiny running stitches (see page 20) along the inner seam line, catch the veiling down from one end of the band to the other.

20 Cut off the excess width of veiling very close to the stitching line along the seam.

Attaching the comb

21 Using a double thread, sew a metal comb in the centre back of the piece and remove the back mark.

22 You've finished!

TIP
Lightly spray the veiling with hairspray to help keep its shape.

FEATHER HAIRBAND

Feathers play a big part in millinery and are a constant source of inspiration for us. Light, feathered pieces are so easy to wear and they won't flatten your hairstyle. This project uses soft, delicate, feathers with an alluring veil just skimming the eyes, and is great for refining your feather-cutting and shaping skills.

You will need:

Sharp scissors
Kettle or hat steamer
Sewing needle
Pins
Thimble
Sewing thread
Tape measure
All-purpose glue
Hairspray
Tissue paper
Curling tongs (optional)

For the feathers:
13–18 pheasant (Lady Amherst)
13–18 pink goose
15–20 single strands of burnt peacock
6–8 striped hackles in both black
    and pink
5–10 guinea fowl
7–10 black goose
5–7 striped coques in both black
    and pink
1 pink curled pheasant quill
1–2 black marabou

For the headpiece:
Alice band and black embroidery
    thread to cover
15 x 10in (38 x 25.5cm) wide
    black veiling

Cutting the feathers

1 Snip off 13 pheasant (Lady Amherst) feathers from the fringe.

2 Take 13 pink goose feathers and cut off the ends where the feathers start to get fluffy.

3 At the stem of all 13 pink goose feathers, dab a tiny bit of glue and stick a Lady Amherst feather on top.

4 Take three of the goose and Lady Amherst feather combinations and stick three strands of burnt peacock, two black striped hackles and one guinea fowl feather at the stem of each.

5 Take one of the feather bunches from step 4 and with a needle and thread, add on two of the pink goose with Lady Amherst feather combinations from step 3 by stitching through the stems and wrapping the thread tightly around to secure. Repeat this to make up three bunches in total.

6 Curl two of the black goose feathers by taking small sections of the feather and with closed scissors curl the ends as if curling gift ribbon for a wrapped present.

7 With a small dab of glue, stick a guinea fowl feather, three strands of burnt peacock and two pink striped hackles at the stem of each black goose feather.

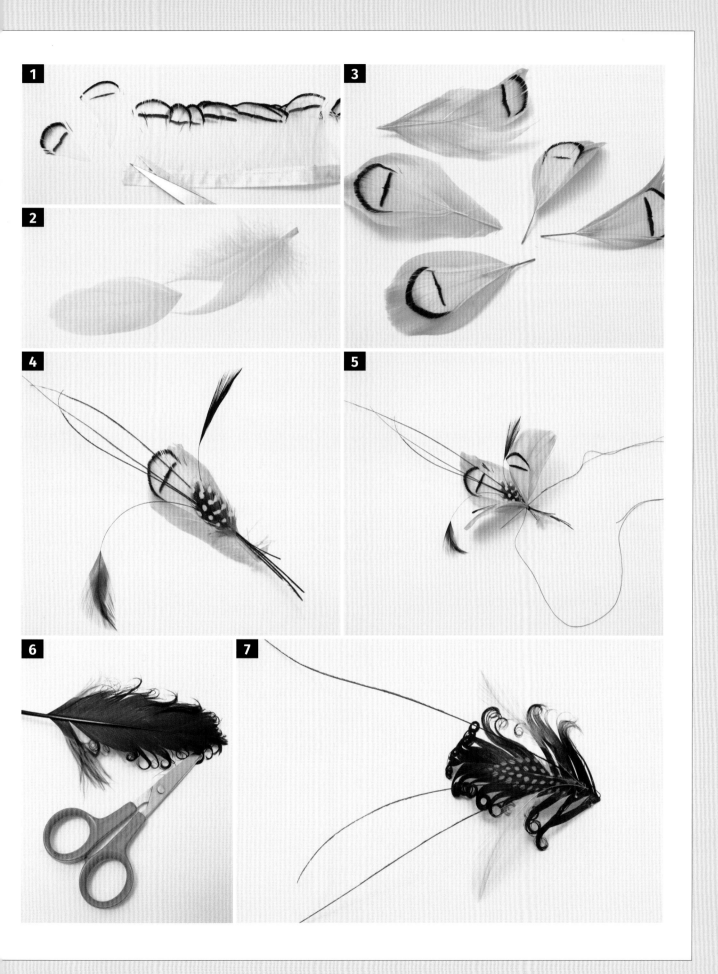

8 Add two of the pink goose and Lady Amherst feather combinations from step 3 to each black goose feather bunch by stitching through the stems, as in step 5. You should now have five bunches of feathers in total.

9 Take a black striped coque feather and snip the end with sharp scissors to create an arrow shape.

10 Approx. 1in (2.5cm) down from the tip of the arrow, pull away and strip off about 1in (2.5cm) of the feather barbs from one side.

11 Snip the feather barbs left at the stem into an arrow shape to match the tip arrow.

12 Repeat step 9 on the other side.

13 Repeat step 10 on the other side. Repeat steps 9–13 with four more of the black striped coque feathers.

14 Take a pink striped coque feather and approx. ⅜in (1cm) from the bottom, cut a curve into the centre, being very careful not to snip the tip off.

15 Using your fingers, strip and pull off the remaining feather from the tip end of the feather down to where you've cut.

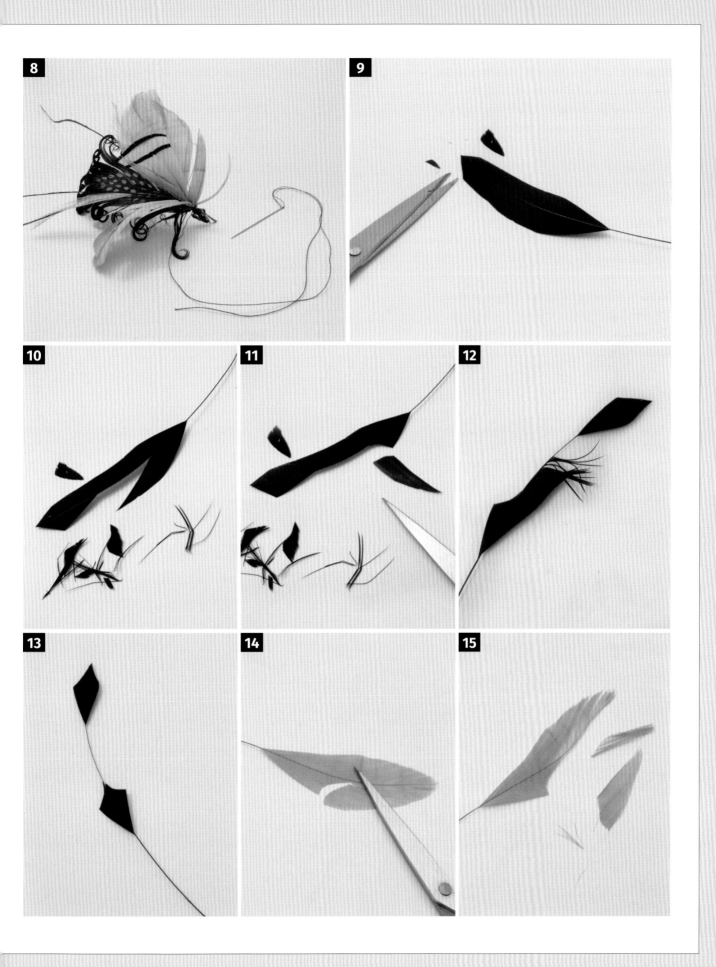

16 Repeat on the other side. On some of the feathers leave a tiny shape of feather on the tip. Repeat steps 14–16 with four more of the pink striped coque feathers.

17 Cut five black goose feathers by snipping an arrow shape at the tip end.

18 About ⅜in (1cm) down from the tip, pull the side of the feather out to form a gap then cut in at an angle.

19 Keep repeating step 18 all the way down the length of feather. When it starts to get fluffy close to the stem, pull the rest of the feather off.

20 Repeat on the other side.

21 Take the five bunches made in steps 1–8 and, at the stem of each bunch, add one black cut striped coque, one pink cut striped coque and one black cut goose feather and sew together as in step 5.

22 You can gently curl the pink goose feathers with curling tongs if you want a more open look. Hold the feather in the tongs for just a few seconds.

23 You should now have five bunches of feathers, two with a black curled goose feather in.

TIP
Hair curling tongs can open and provide a beautiful curl to feathers.

Making the veiling

24 Cover an Alice band in black embroidery thread (see page 34).

25 Measure 3in (7.5cm) up both sides of the ends of the Alice band and mark with a pin.

26 Take the piece of veiling and measure 7in (18cm) up from the centre of the bottom edge and mark with a pin. From one side, run a gathering thread in a curve to this pin mark (see page 20), leaving an end to pull. Repeat on the other side.

27 Pin the ends of both sides of the veiling onto the Alice band and pin the centre of the veiling (where the gathering threads end) to the centre of the Alice band.

28 Gently pull both gathering lines to evenly distribute the veiling then pin it onto the Alice band between the pin marks all along the hairband.

29 Pull out the gathering threads and sew a neat running stitch (see page 20), catching the veiling down along the Alice band.

30 Carefully cut the excess veiling off the Alice band.

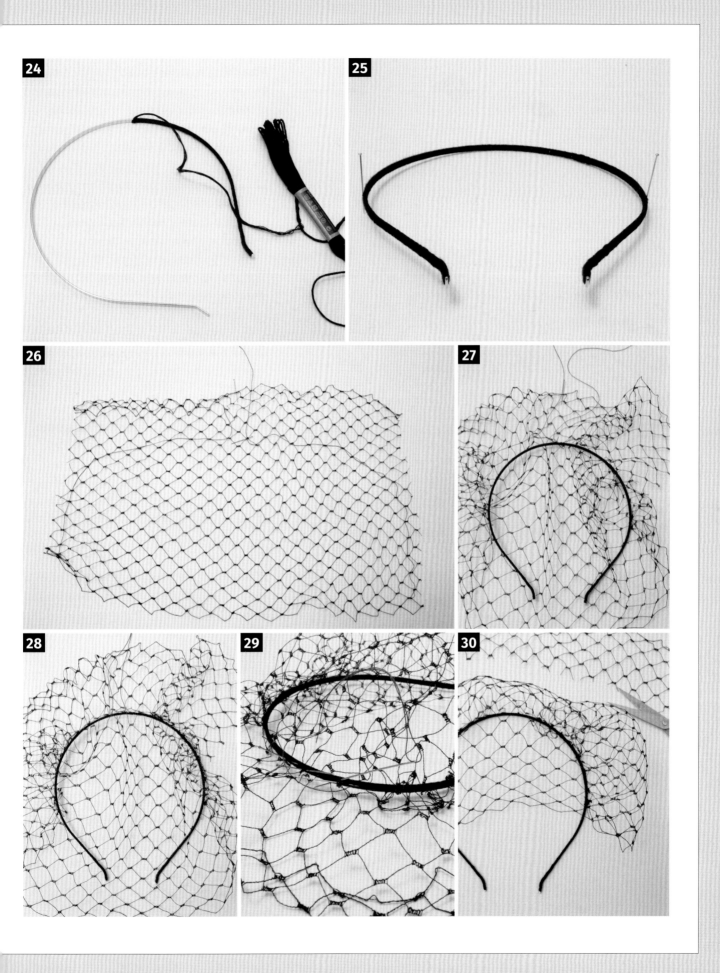

Attaching feathers onto the Alice band

31 Measure approx. 5½in (14cm) from the end of the Alice band on the right side. At this position, pin on a feather bunch and sew on securely with double thread.

32 Take a second feather bunch and place the end of the stem at a right angle next to the first feather bunch. Pin in place and sew securely onto the Alice band.

33 Place the third feather bunch at the base of the last bunch facing towards the veiling and sew on securely.

34 Sew the fourth feather bunch on the Alice band facing down the right side of the band.

35 Sew the fifth bunch of feathers in the middle of the others to face out at the back of the head.

36 Now sew in the pink curled pheasant quill to sit on the top of where all the bunches of feathers have been sewn on, so that it's curling out nicely at the top.

37 Now fill in any gaps where feathers have been sewn onto the Alice band with any leftover feathers and a few snipped little pieces of black marabou. Use tiny dabs of all-purpose glue to secure stems that are too fine to sew.

38 Pad out the veiling with tissue paper. Wave in the steam from a kettle for a few seconds. When dry, spray the veiling with hairspray, then leave to set for a bit before taking the tissue pad out.

39 You can gently curve any of the striped coque feathers in curling tongs if they need it. You've finished!

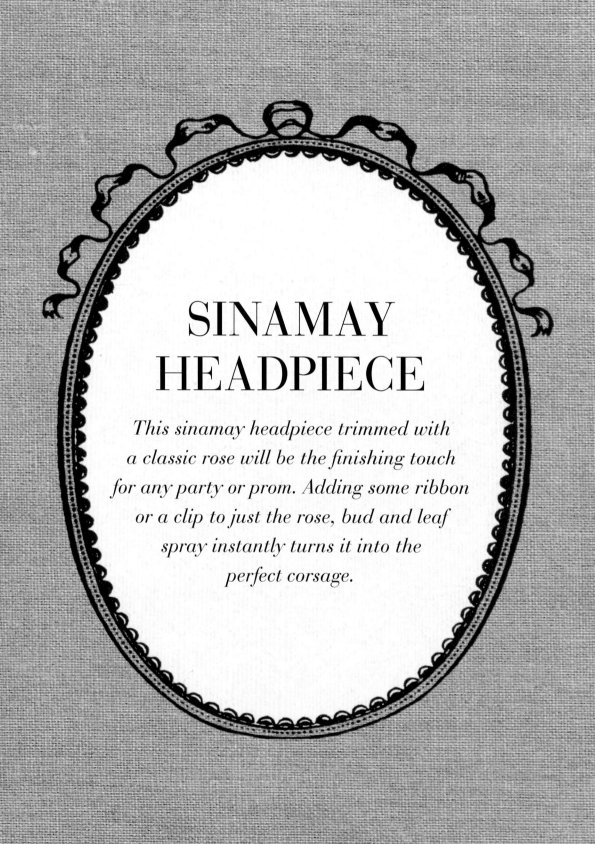

SINAMAY HEADPIECE

This sinamay headpiece trimmed with a classic rose will be the finishing touch for any party or prom. Adding some ribbon or a clip to just the rose, bud and leaf spray instantly turns it into the perfect corsage.

You will need:

The patterns for the petals
Pliers with a cutting edge
Matching paint, ink or felt-tip pen
Needles
Pins
Thimble
Sewing thread in colours to match
    chosen fabrics
Tape measure
Scissors
Iron and ironing board
All-purpose glue
Firm-hold hairspray
Bradawl

For the base and loops:
14in (35.5cm) length of US 16 gauge
    (SWG18, 1.2mm) millinery wire
12 x 6in (30.5 x 15cm) bias strip
    of pre-stiffened sinamay
25 x 3in (63.5 x 7.5cm) bias strip
    of pre-stiffened sinamay
16 x 3in (40.5 x 7.5cm) bias strip
    of pre-stiffened sinamy
Alice band and embroidery thread
    to cover

For the rose, bud and leaves:
25in (63.5cm) length of 26 gauge
    (SWG 27, 0.4mm) millinery wire
34 x 2½in (86.5 x 6.5cm) duchess
    satin (this does not need to be one
    continuous strip)
4 x 4in (10 x 10cm) duchess satin
13 x 3in (33 x 7.5cm) bias strip
    of organza
6½ x 3in (16.5 x 7.5cm) strip of
    adhesive web
1¼in (3cm) paper ball

Making the disc

1 Join the wire with a 2in (5cm) overlap (see page 27) and shape to make a circle. Colour to match your chosen sinamay with either paint, coloured ink or a felt-tip pen.

2 Fold the 12 x 6in (30.5 x 15cm) bias strip of sinamay in half so that you have two layers of sinamay that are 6 x 6in (15 x 15cm). Place the wire circle onto the sinamay and pin the wire and the sinamay together.

3 Trim the sinamay back to ½in (1.5cm) from the wire edge all the way around the disc.

4 Fold the turning over the wire, re-pinning as you go to hold it in place.

5 Using a double thread, sew the edge down close to the wire using a stab stitch (see page 18). Use a tiny stitch on the right side and a longer one on the underneath side.

6 Trim the turning back to approx. ¼in (0.6cm).

7 Opposite the join in the wire, mark the front with a tie tack (see page 19) in a contrasting coloured thread (you can estimate this by eye). Pop a pin in the back and at both sides.

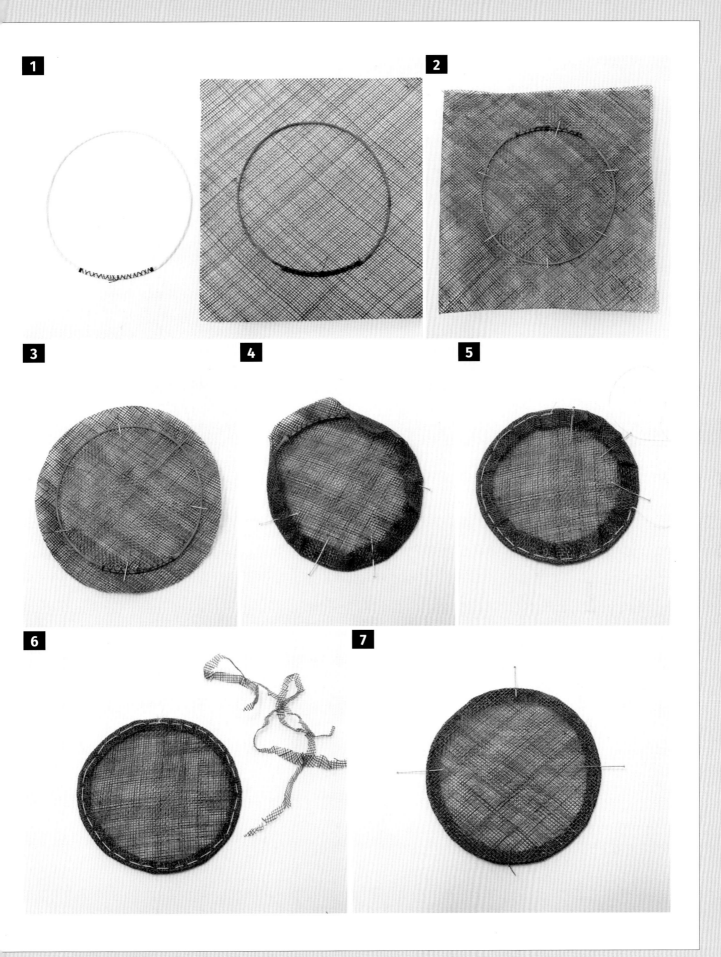

1

2

3

4

5

6

7

8 Mark the covered Alice band (see page 34) by catching the thread with a pin 7in (18cm) from one end. This mark will be slightly off centre.

9 With the pin marking the back of the sinamay base at 12 o'clock, place your 3 o'clock pin next to the pin marking 7in (18cm) on the Alice band and attach securely (see page 35).

10 Attach the 9 o'clock pin to the Alice band where it falls comfortably. The measurement to this end of the Alice band will be approx. 4¼in (11.5cm).

Making the loops

11 Take the 25in (63.5cm) bias strip of sinamay and cut in half to form two 12½ x 3in (32 x 7.5cm) strips, then do the same with the 16in (40.5cm) strip to form two 8 x 3in (20 x 7.5cm) strips. Make a 1in (2.5cm) turning on all four strips on one long side only and press with an iron.

12 Fold over and iron once more so that you have four strips of sinamay, each with three layers, each strip 1in (2.5cm) wide.

13 Join the ends of each strip together to make four circles using a tiny stab stitch (see page 18) and a ½in (1.5cm) overlap. The raw edge from the second fold should be on the inside of the circle.

14 Pin the four loops towards the back and the left hand side of the simanay disc in a pleasing arrangement. You may want to keep them as circles or squash them a little to make ovals. When you are happy with the arrangement, sew them on using small stab stitches (see page 18), going all the way through the loops and into the disc. Put to one side while you make the rose, bud and leaf trim.

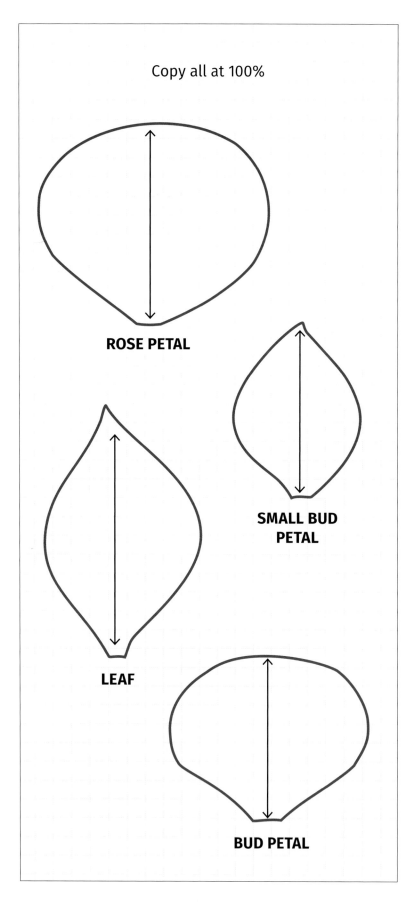

Copy all at 100%

ROSE PETAL

SMALL BUD PETAL

LEAF

BUD PETAL

Making the rose

15 Dye the wire with green-coloured ink, paint or a felt-tip pen. Cut a 5in (12.5cm) length and make a turning at one end of 1in (2.5cm).

16 Transfer the patterns onto paper (see page 35) and cut out eight rose petals, one bud petal and four small bud petals from the strip of duchess satin.

17 Saturate all the petals with hairspray and leave to dry. Shape the eight rose petals by manipulating the fabric to create dents and randomly curled edges. Give each of the rose petals a small pleat at its base and lightly spray with hairspray to fix. Put one rose petal to one side with the bud petal and the four small bud petals.

18 Take one of the petals and make a gentle fold approximately ½in (1.5cm) from the top edge. Wrap it around the 1in (2.5cm) end of double wire, ensuring you cover the wire completely. Stitch in place using tiny stab stitches (see page 18).

19 Gather the remaining part of the petal around the wire, then stitch and wrap to secure.

20 Choose the next petal and place on top of the first, but to one side, in such a position so that it starts to create the centre of the rose. Stitch securely to the first petal.

21 Continue building the rose in the same way, keeping it well balanced and aiming for a slightly oval shape.

22 Spray the whole rose with hairspray to fix. There should be one petal left over from step 17 for use later.

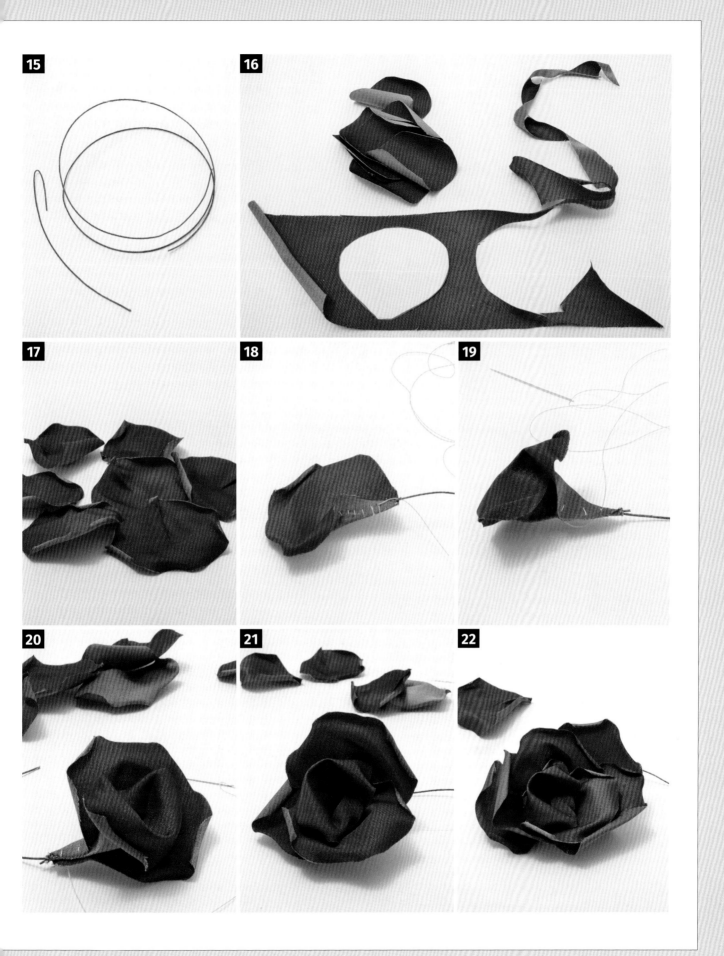

Making the bud

23 Make a hole about halfway up through the centre of the paper ball with the bradawl. Cut 5in (12.5cm) of green wire. Put a blob of all-purpose glue on one end of the wire and push it up into the ball and leave to dry.

24 Using the square of satin, cover the ball by stitching and wrapping with a double thread at the base of the ball. Keep the gathers as evenly spread out as possible.

25 Trim away the excess fabric close to the thread.

26 Stick the four small bud petals to the base of the covered ball, covering up the gathers and the trimmed-back fabric.

27 Shape the bud petal in the same way as the rose petals, creating dents and randomly curled edges, and stick to the base of the bud. Spray the whole bud with hairspray to fix.

Making the leaves

28 Lay the strip of adhesive web on top of the bias strip of organza. Lay three 5in (12.5cm) pieces of green wire on top of the adhesive web, checking there is enough space for each leaf, and with the end of the wire approx. ¾in (2cm) from the edge of the organza. Make a sandwich of the wires by bringing the other side of the organza strip over and pressing according to the instructions on the adhesive web.

29 Using the leaf pattern, cut out three leaves.

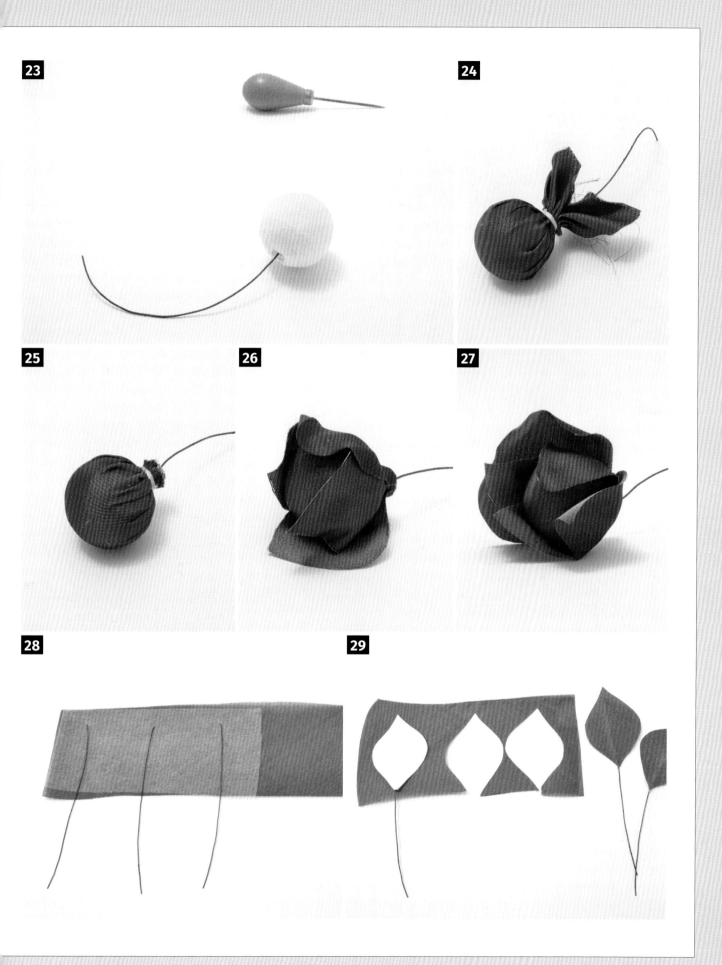

TIP
If you want to make a larger headpiece,
cut out the sinamay a little wider and
longer for bigger loops and add a few
more petals or buds and leaves.

30 Cut little nicks in the edges of the leaves
to give them a serrated-looking edge. Using
an iron on a medium heat, warm the leaves
then make gentle scores down the central
vein and out towards the edges of the leaf
on both sides using the bradawl.

31 Bend the wires to make the leaves look
more realistic then spray them with hairspray
to fix.

32 Collect together all the elements you
have made.

33 Pin the flower on to the disc slightly right
of centre and sew by using a stab stitch (see
page 18), going all the way through the base
of the flower and the sinamay disc.

34 Stitch the bud to the sinamay base in the
same way. Place it to the left of the rose.

35 Stitch the leaves to the base by oversewing
the wires securely (see page 27). Stitch two
of the leaves on the right-hand side and one
in between the bud and rose.

36 Sew the extra petal to the right of the
rose, filling in the gap and covering where the
piece is attached to the Alice band. If there
are any other gaps you feel you should fill,
just make up some more petals.

37 Arrange the leaves as in the photograph
or however looks best when it is being worn.
You've finished!

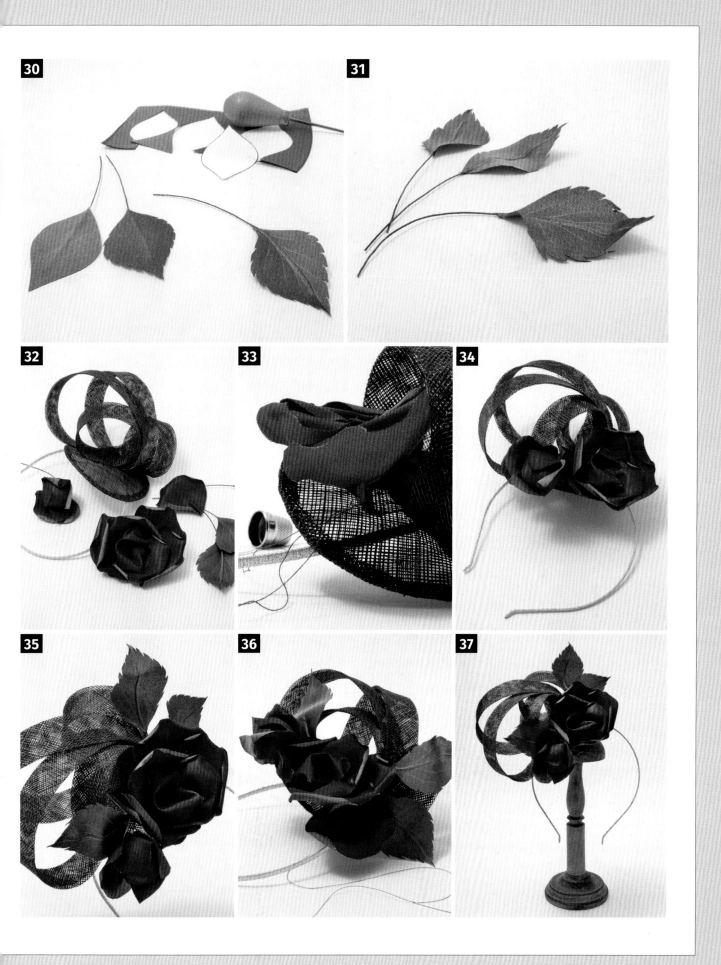

FELT TRILBY

We are aware that not every home milliner has access to blocks so we have created this classic trilby shape using just a standard dome block and a flat pattern for its brim. Combining traditional petersham ribbon with contemporary colours makes this a trilby with a twist!

You will need:

The pattern for the brim
Needles
Pins (blocking and dressmaking)
Thimble
Sewing thread in colour to match felt
Dome block
Food wrap
Sticky tape
Blocking cord
Felt stiffener and paintbrush
Tape measure
Scissors
Pliers with a cutting edge
Iron and ironing board
Kettle or hat steamer
Small piece of cotton cloth
Bowl of water
Small clothes brush
All-purpose glue

For the hat:
Velour felt capeline
36in (91.5cm) length of US 16 gauge
    (SWG 18, 1.2mm) white millinery wire

For the trim:
10in (25.5cm) lengths of no. 5 petersham
    ribbons in four different colours
23½in (59.5cm) length of no. 5
    petersham ribbon in colour to match
    felt for head fitting
59in (150cm) length of no. 3 petersham
    ribbon in colour to match felt

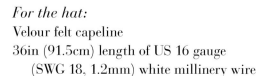

TIP

Cutting snips in the seam allowance on the pattern will help
you to shape it more easily onto the felt before cutting out.

Cutting the brim

1 Transfer the brim pattern piece on page 86 to paper (see page 35) and cut out. Snip into the seam allowance with approx. ⅜in (1cm) spaces then pin the pattern at the bottom of the crown, where it naturally sits, and cut out. The slight curve where the crown goes into the brim makes the perfect curve for the head fitting.

2 Put a front mark (see page 21) on the outside edge of the brim and run a tacking line (see page 20) around the head fitting. Snip into the head fitting seam allowance as before with approximately 1in (2.5cm) spaces.

Shaping the crown

3 Cover your block with food wrap and secure underneath with sticky tape (see page 23). Steam the crown of the velour capeline until nice and soft and damp. Pull it over the dome so it sits snug and flat against the block, then secure it with pins around the edge and strong nylon cord (see page 25). Leave to dry.

4 While the crown is drying, place the right sides of the brim piece together and whip stitch the back seam (see page 20).

5 When the crown is dry, put a front and back mark in at the bottom of the crown and take it off the block. Brush a light, even layer of felt stiffener onto the inside of the crown (see page 17).

6 Put the crown back on the block but lift it up approximately 1½in (4cm) from the bottom edge, so it won't fit the block now. To secure it in place, pin the sides, front and back then add four more pins in between the first four, evenly spaced.

7 To make the indentation on the top, gently push the top of the felt down in a teardrop shape, with the point of the teardrop shape to the centre front, and pin to the block.

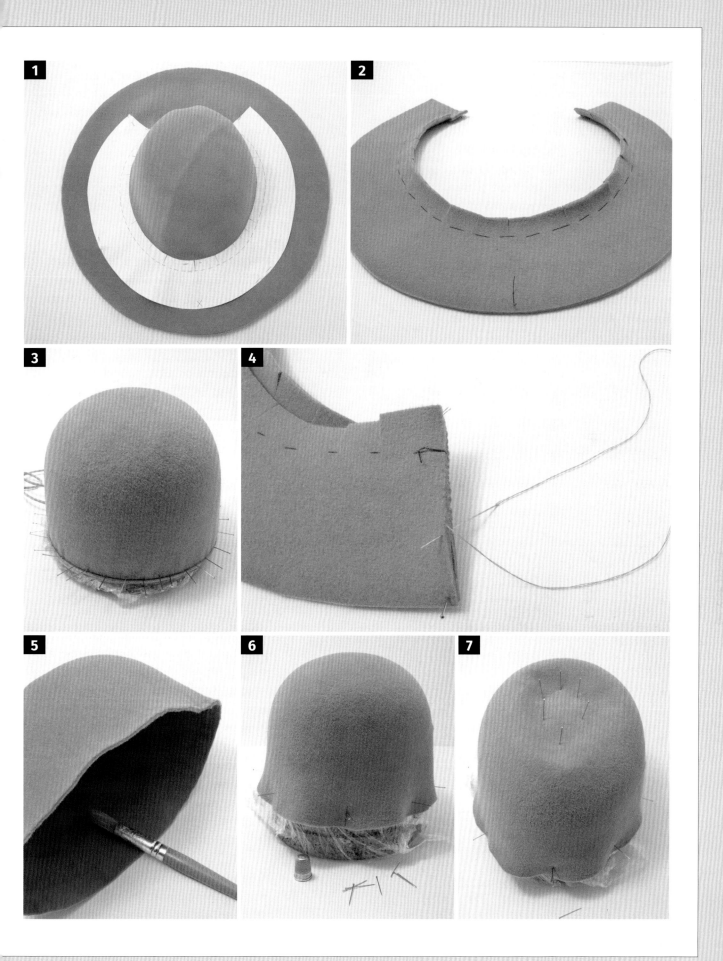

8 To make the front indentations near the top of the dome, gently push in the sides of the felt to create two egg-like shapes the same size and evenly spaced from the centre front. Give a light steam and leave to dry. When it's dry, take the pins out of the bottom edge and while it's still on the block even up the bottom edge with scissors so you have a nice straight line. This will only be a minute amount. Check both the side measurements are the same from the tip of the crown to the bottom edge and your front and back edges are even. You can now take the crown off the block and set to one side.

Shaping and trimming the brim

9 Put the brim on the dome block, matching the front mark to the block front mark. Secure with a few pins then flip the back seam up.

10 Take out some of the curve from the millinery wire (see page 26). Sew the wire just inside the top of the felt edge with blanket stitch (see page 27).

11 Follow the curve of the brim and when joining the wire at the back, pull the wire in gently to keep the back of the felt flipping up. The overlap in wire should be approx. 3in (7.5cm).

12 Cut approx. 34in (86.5cm) no. 3 petersham ribbon and fold it in half lengthways, using your fingertips to make a gentle crease along the fold.

13 Starting at the back of the brim, ¼in (0.6cm) to the left of the back seam, pin the fold of the petersham ribbon over the edge of the brim, pulling it taut as you go around. When you reach the back again, fold over ¼in (0.6cm) of the petersham ribbon on top of where you started to match up with the back seam. Secure with tacking stitches (see page 20).

14 Sew the petersham ribbon onto the edge of the brim. Use tiny stab stitches (see page 18) going all the way through the felt, catching the petersham ribbon on both the right and the wrong side of the brim. Insert your needle at an angle for all stitches as you move along.

15 Run a small damp cloth around the petersham ribbon; this will shrink it in between the stitches so that it fits the edge beautifully and gives it a nice finish. The cloth should just be a little damp and not too wet.

16 Sew in a no. 5 petersham ribbon to fit your head size along the tacking line on the brim (see page 30), then take the tacking line out.

BRIM
Copy at 350%

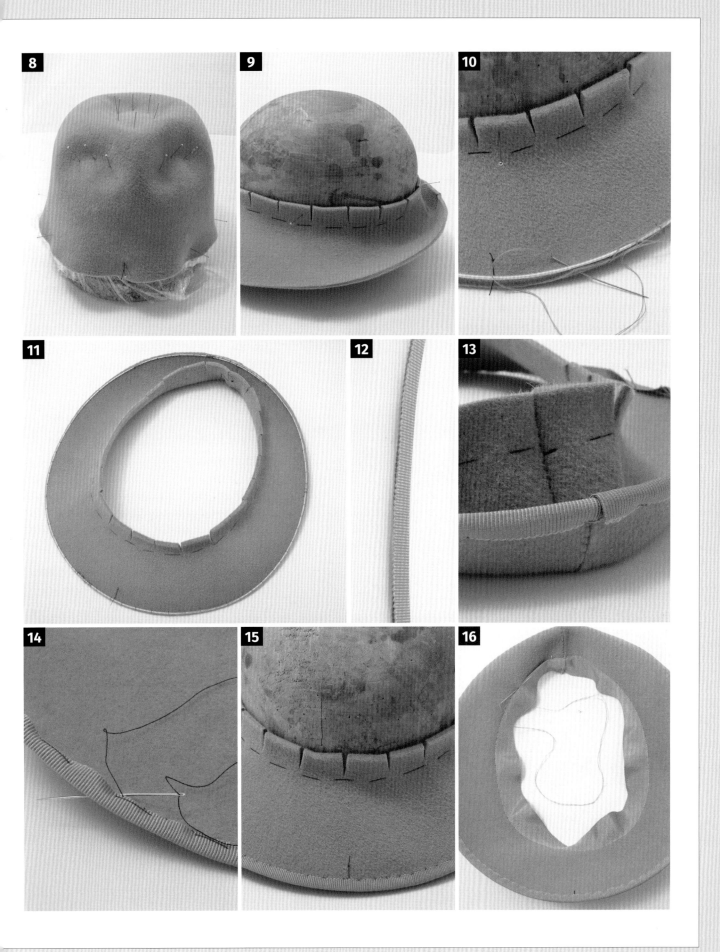

Joining the brim and crown

17 Take the crown off the block and place it on top of the head-fitting allowance on the brim. Pull the petersham ribbon down inside so it's out of the way and pin the crown onto the brim. Start with joining up the front and back marks then the sides, then pin in between these so the crown is evenly distributed.

18 As the hat has a narrow trimming and you don't want any stitches to show we're using a running stitch here (see page 20) rather than the normal backstitch. Use a double thread in the felt colour (shown in black thread in the photo to be clearer) and have the longer running stitch inside the hat and a tiny stitch on the outside that will be covered with petersham trims. Evenly space the stitches and take the pins out as you go around. Flip the head-fitting petersham ribbon inside the hat back up to cover the stitches.

19 Hold a small clothes brush in some steam then brush over where the crown is sewn onto the brim to soften any marks where the stitches are. It's worth also brushing all over the crown to remove any pin marks made by blocking.

Adding the trim

20 Cut a 2in (5cm) piece of no. 5 petersham ribbon and fold the two top corners into the centre. Make sure these two raw edges don't overlap the bottom edge of the petersham.

21 Fold the two bottom corners into the centre and do a tiny invisible stab stitch (see page 18) on each point to keep it in place. Make up five of these in each colour of petersham ribbon.

22 Take your leftover no. 3 petersham ribbon, fold it in half lengthways and iron it flat. Place the five petersham trims in a line so the point of each trim is touching the last one to avoid gaps. Sew them on with a tiny stab stitch just where the folded corners meet so the point is left free.

23 Keep repeating the same order of colours until the band is full.

24 Remove the front marks from the crown and the brim. Pull down the head-fitting petersham ribbon inside the hat to keep it out of the way while you are sewing the petersham trimming band on. Place the band around the hat, starting at the centre back seam and covering the raw felt edge. Pin in place. Sew the band on with tiny stab stitches underneath the trims so the stitches are hidden. When you reach the other end, fold the end of the narrow band over to hide the raw edge. If you have a gap at the back, make up one more petersham trim to fill it.

25 You've finished!

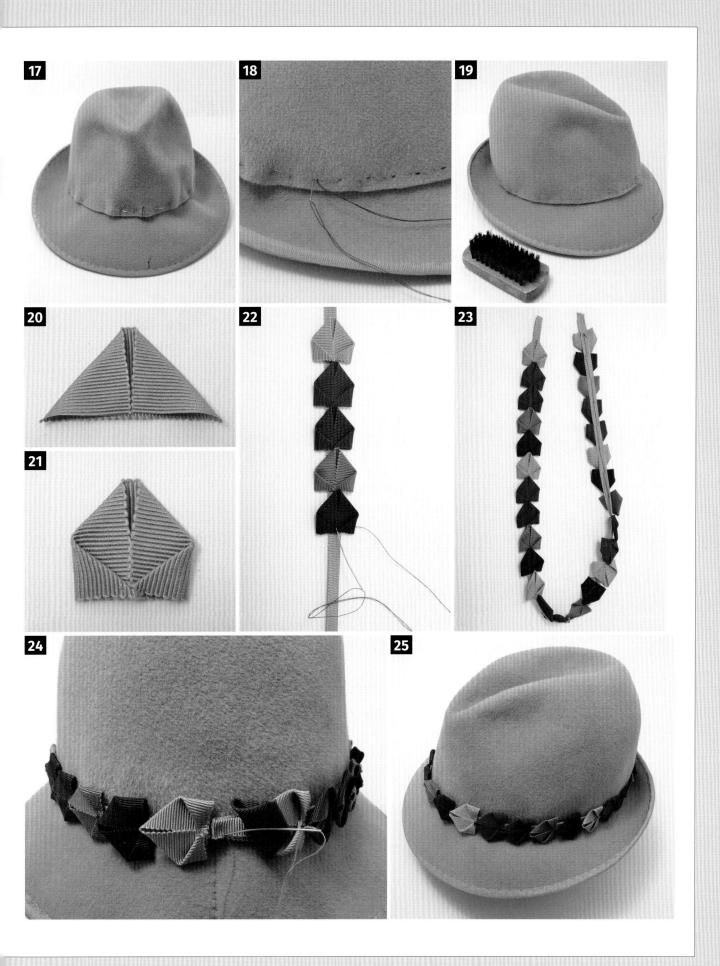

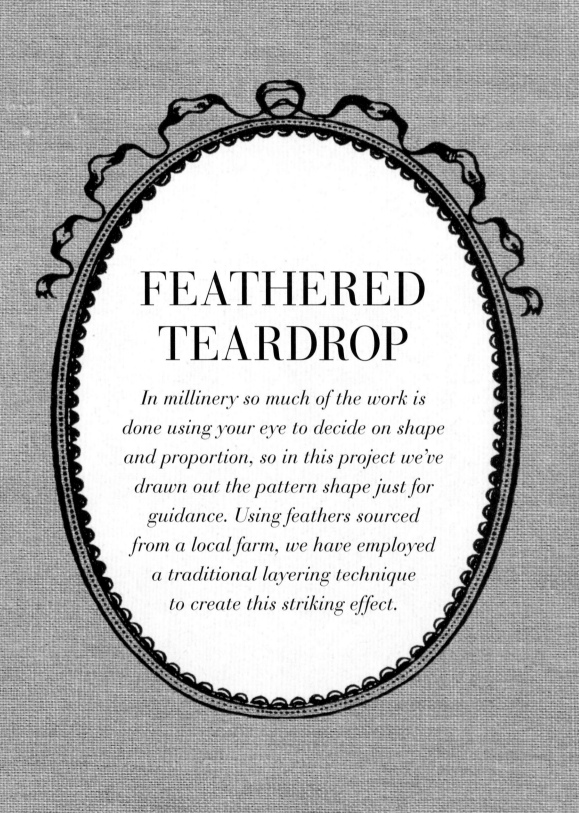

FEATHERED TEARDROP

In millinery so much of the work is done using your eye to decide on shape and proportion, so in this project we've drawn out the pattern shape just for guidance. Using feathers sourced from a local farm, we have employed a traditional layering technique to create this striking effect.

You will need:

The teardrop pattern
Dome block
Food wrap
Sticky tape
Pliers with a cutting edge
Needles
Pins (blocking and dressmaking)
Thimble
Sewing thread in colour to match felt
Tape measure
Scissors
All-purpose glue
Black or brown pen
White pencil (optional)
Kettle or hat steamer

For the hat:
Wool felt cone in dark grey
24in (61cm) length of US 16 gauge
    (SWG 18, 1.2mm) millinery wire
Alice band and embroidery thread
    to cover to match feathers

For the feathers:
39in (1m) of collared pheasant plumage
1 black quill
1 brown tigered quill

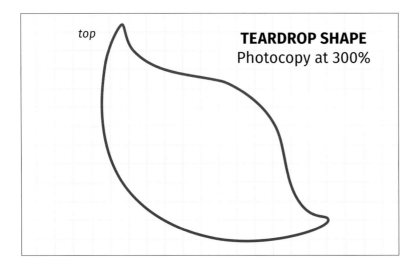

Shaping the felt

1 Cover the dome block with some food wrap and secure underneath with sticky tape. Cut a rectangular piece of felt from the bottom of the cone approx. 11in (28cm) in length by 6in (15cm) in width. Block this onto the dome block and leave to dry (see page 25).

2 When it's dry, take out the pins from one side of the felt and flip this side up. Transfer the teardrop shape pattern onto paper (see page 35) then place it onto the felt, marking with a pin line where you would like it to go. The shape measures approx. 9in (23cm) in length and 5½in (14cm) in width at its widest part where the back starts curving up.

3 Take the rest of the pins out of the block and try the shape on your head in front of a mirror to check the lines are to your liking. Make any adjustments with the pins and when you're happy with the shape, draw on with a white pencil or sew a tacking line.

Adding the wire

4 Starting on the right side where your join will be, shape the wire with your fingertips to the line, making sure your wire is curved nicely where the felt flips up. Pin in place.

5 Take the wire off the felt and join the ends.

6 Pin the wire onto the underside of the felt following the white pencil line from the other side. Sew the wire on with blanket stitch.

7 Cut around the edge of the felt following the wire shape and leaving a ⅜in (1cm) seam allowance to be turned over the wire.

8 Hold the edge of the felt in steam to soften the seam allowance so you can fold it over the wire. If your turning is too wide, trim off a bit more. At the pointed ends, mitre the corners by cutting off the excess felt to allow the edges to meet and sit neat and flat.

top

TEARDROP SHAPE
Photocopy at 300%

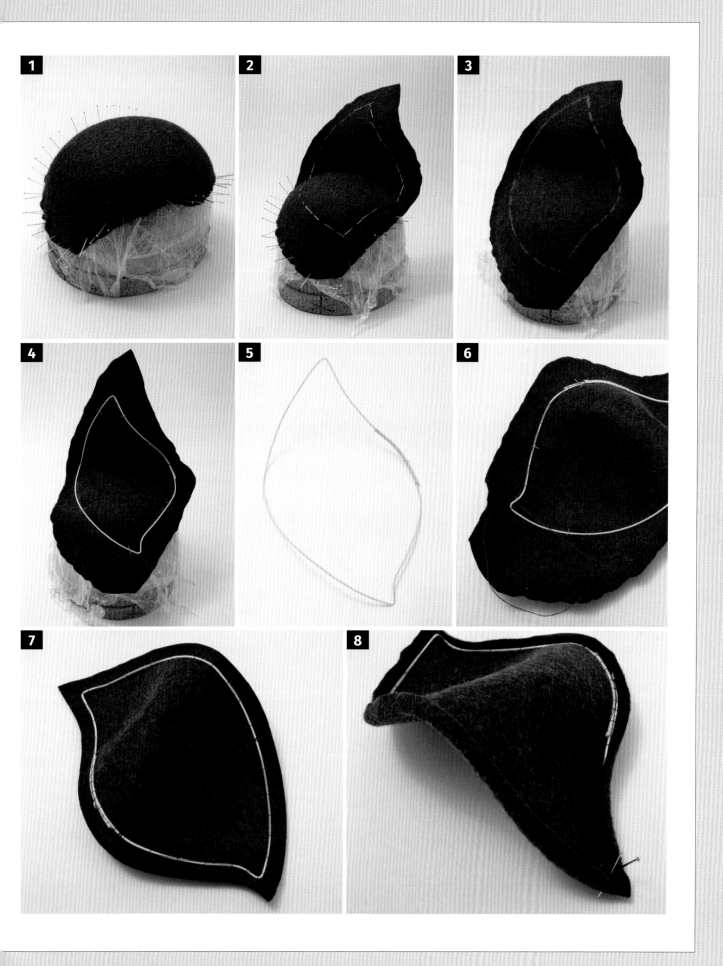

9 Sew the turning down with a stab stitch (see page 18), pulling the mitred corners together. Pull the thread taut so your stitches sink into the felt making them invisible.

Attaching the Alice band

10 Cover an Alice band with embroidery thread (see page 34). Measure approx. 6½in (16.5cm) up from the end of the right side on the Alice band and insert a pin. Measure approx. 3½in (9cm) up from the left side on the Alice band and insert another pin. Pin the felt shape onto the Alice band where the pin marks are. The pins should meet the edge of the hat. Try it on in a mirror to check the positioning is to your liking. Using a thread colour to match the Alice band, sew the band securely onto the felt using double thread going over the band. It doesn't matter if your stitches are showing on the right side of the hat as they will be covered with feathers.

TIP

Try making this hat in another feather design of your choice.

Adding the feathers

11 Prepare your feathers by snipping off the ends where the feather starts to get fluffy and where the feather pattern stops.

12 On the bottom edge, start your first line of feathers. Put a thin bit of glue onto the felt and place the first feather on the bottom point so that it is partly coming off the edge. Put another thin bit of glue on top approx. ½in (1.5cm) from the feather tip and lay the next feather on. Leave equal distances from each tip of the feather.

13 Carry on in this way following the edge to the top point.

14 Start your next row of feathers at the bottom point next to the first row. Carry on up to the top following the first line of feathers.

15 Continue laying the feathers in this way, following your last line. You may need to fill in with smaller feathers where the felt curves up.

16 When completing the last line, curve the feathers over the edge a little. All your edges should be nice and feathery with no felt showing. You may like to feather the back as well or leave the contrast of the felt showing.

Adding the quills

17 Securely sew on the two quills in a place you like, sewing through the side of the quill so your stitches don't show.

18 Hold the top end of the quills in some steam to give a gentle curl following the line of the hat. Cut the bottom ends of quills down on an angle if too long. If the quill is left white on the end where you've cut it off, touch it up with a black or brown pen. You've finished!

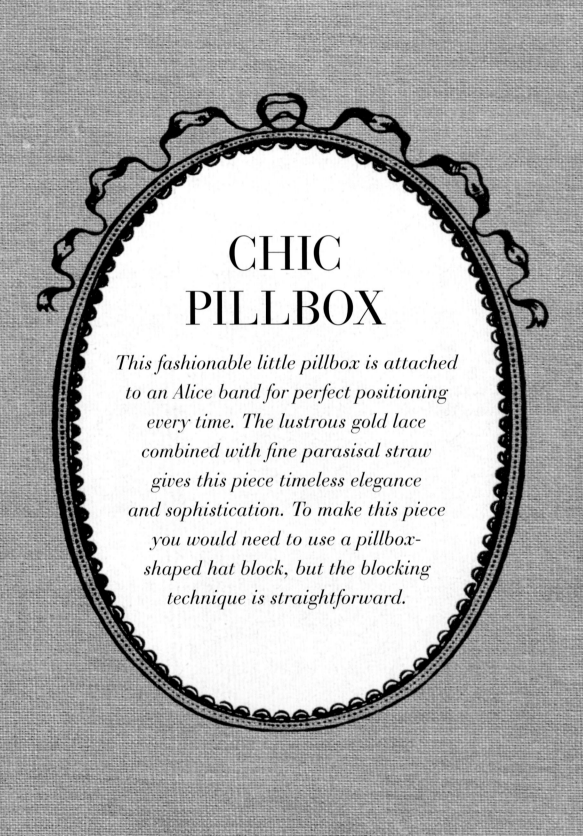

CHIC PILLBOX

This fashionable little pillbox is attached to an Alice band for perfect positioning every time. The lustrous gold lace combined with fine parasisal straw gives this piece timeless elegance and sophistication. To make this piece you would need to use a pillbox-shaped hat block, but the blocking technique is straightforward.

You will need:

Pillbox-shaped block
Food wrap
Sticky tape
Breadboard or flat surface
Needles and pins (blocking and
    dressmaking)
Thimble
Cream colour sewing thread and a
    tacking thread in contrast colour
Tape measure
Scissors
Iron and ironing board
Pressing cloth (organza or light
    cotton fabric)
Pressing pad
Corsetry boning or palette knife
Straw stiffener and brush
All-purpose glue
Water spray bottle or damp cloth
Kettle or hat steamer

For the hat:
Parasisal straw cone in cream colour
Approx. 51¼ x 3in (130 x 7.5cm)
    gold lace braid
Approx. 32 x 4in (81 x 10cm) lightweight
    adhesive web
Alice band and embroidery thread
    to cover
23in (58.5cm) length of no. 3 cream
    petersham ribbon
20 x 4½in (51 x 11.5cm) bias strip
    of cream lining
9 x 9in (23 x 23cm) square of
    cream lining
Button trimming (e.g. an old brooch)

NB: Amounts listed here are to fit pillbox
block measurements 11in (28cm)
front-to-back (including turning) x 10in
(25.5cm) side-to-side (including turning).

Making the straw pillbox

1 Cover your block with food wrap and secure underneath with sticky tape (see page 23). The purpose of covering your block is so your straw doesn't stick to it, so make sure there are no gaps in the food wrap.

2 Dampen the straw cone with water using a water spray bottle or damp cloth but make sure you don't saturate it.

3 Pull the cone over the block and pin securely in four equal spaced places at 2 o'clock, 4 o'clock, 7 o'clock and 10 o'clock. Make sure the tip of your cone where the weave starts is right in the centre of the block. You want the weave pattern to be in a diamond shape to your centre front.

4 Smooth out the straw as much as possible so there are no bumps or bubbles, working the straw over to the underside, and pin all around the edge so it's nice and smooth with no gathers. If you have any little bumps left in the four ends of the diamond shape don't worry – as the straw dries these will shrink to nothing and become smooth. Leave it to dry now for a few hours or overnight.

5 If there are any tiny bumps once the straw is dry, you can press them out with your iron on medium-hot heat and a pressing cloth between the iron and straw. (The pressing cloth keeps the straw nice and clean by preventing any marks from the iron transferring onto your hat.)

6 Cut the excess straw off under your pin line (if your pins are in the way remove them before cutting and put them back afterwards).

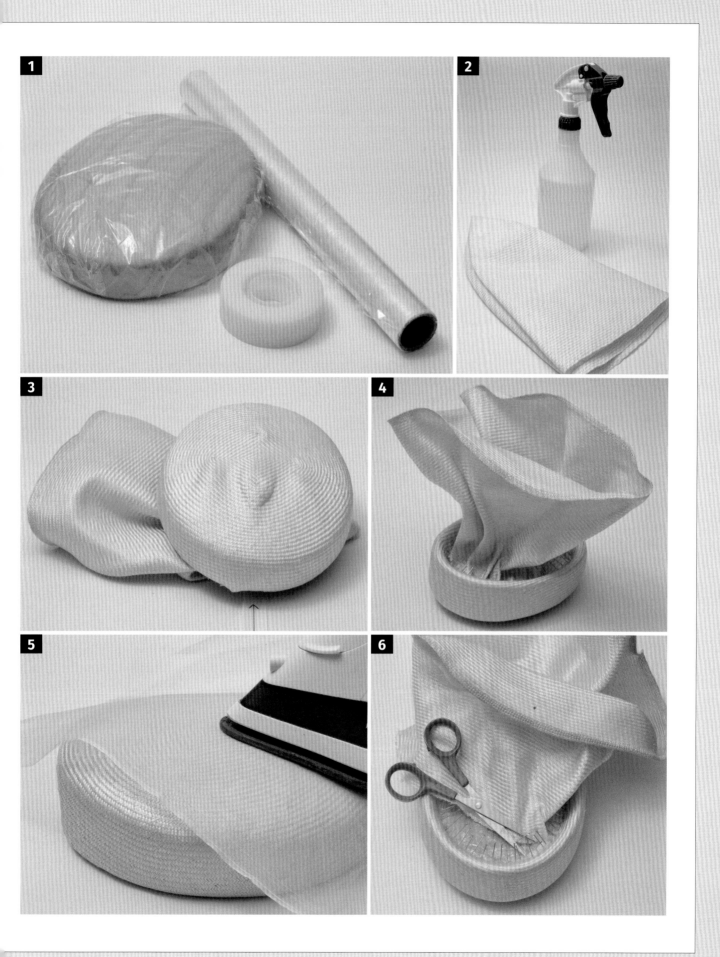

7 Using straw stiffener, give the cone an even covering, working the stiffener into the straw and making sure you go just over your pin line. When dipping your brush into the stiffener, squeeze the excess off the brush on the side of the jar so it's not too wet, otherwise your hat will dry too hard. Leave to dry for couple of hours.

8 Take all the pins out using pliers if they're stuck. Gently slip the corsetry boning or palette knife inside the straw, running it around the edge and easing the straw off the block without misshaping it.

9 Sew a front and back mark in.

TIP

If you are using a deeper shaped pillbox, your braid will need to be wider. Make sure the pattern in the braid is sitting straight around the straw.

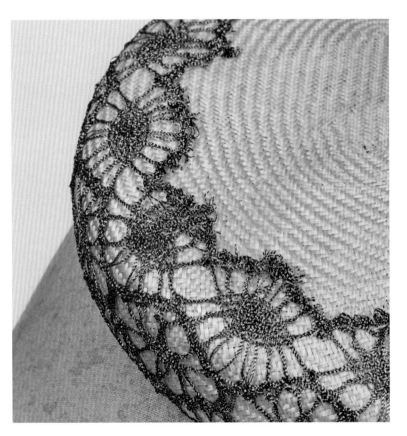

Adding the braid

10 Start pinning the braid onto the block at about ten past two from the centre back. This is where the trimming will be attached so it will cover up the join in the braid. The braiding needs to be blocked before it goes onto the straw to give it a better fitting and shape.

11 Carry on gently easing on and pinning where needed, making sure the braid sits snugly to the block.

12 Check that you are keeping the pattern in the braid straight and taking enough over the underside of block so the petersham ribbon will cover it. Cut and finish it off, joining where you started. Wave the blocked braid in some steam for a few seconds – this will set the braid to help keep its shape.

13 After you've let the braid dry to set it (around 20 minutes), you can carefully unpin it from the block and lay it around your straw in the same position as you pinned it onto the block, i.e. starting at ten past two from the centre back.

14 Using a cream single thread with a knot, start to stab stitch (see page 18) from the join, working your way around the shape in a zig-zag pattern from the braid on the top of the hat down to the inside edge. Use tiny stabs on the lace about 1in (2.5cm) inside the hat.

15 Make sure your stab stitches go right up to your raw edge of straw inside the pillbox.

16 Sew in the petersham ribbon with single cream thread (see page 30).

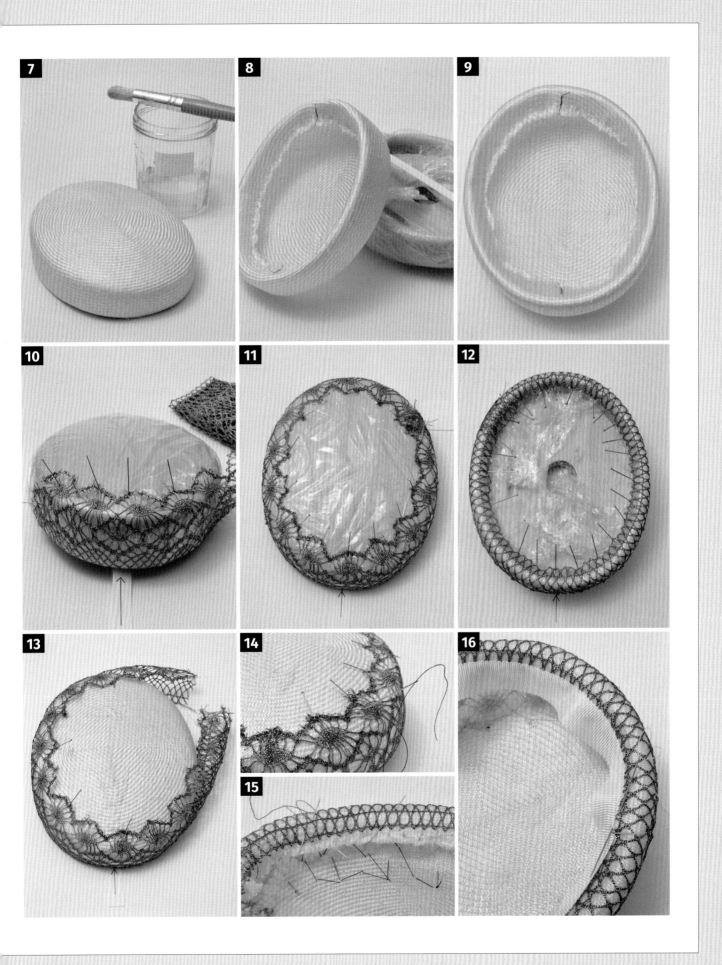

Making the loop trimming

17 Take the piece of straw that was cut off the pillbox earlier. Cut up one side of it along the fold.

18 Cover a flat breadboard or other flat surface with food wrap. Dampen the straw with water spray and pin it onto the surface. You will probably need to do this in two stages if your breadboard isn't long enough. Put enough pins in to pull the straw along the grain so it's sitting really taut and flat. Leave to dry.

19 Press the straw with a medium-hot iron with the steam on and a pressing cloth in between the iron and the straw as before.

20 Stiffen as you did before (see step 7), applying the same amount of stiffener. Leave to dry.

21 Unpin the straw from your flat surface. Start by pinning a line of pins along the length about 1in (2.5cm) from the edge. From this line, measure up 1½in (4cm) and do a second line of pins. Now run a tacking line in a contrast colour so it shows up along each line of pins (see page 20). Take the pins out.

22 Measure ⅜in (1cm) outwards from both tacking lines and run a row of pins along; this is to form the seam allowance that will be turned along both edges. Cut along both pin lines to cut off the excess straw.

23 Turn the length of straw so the wrong side is facing up. Using your fingers, turn over half the seam allowance all the way along the edge so it meets the tacking line. Press with an iron using a pressing cloth.

24 Now turn the same edge over again to form a nice straight line along the whole length of straw. Press with an iron using a pressing cloth. Repeat steps 22 and 23 again on the other side of straw. Take the tacking stitches out.

25 Using single cream thread, sew along both your turned edges using a stab stitch, shown here in black thread to be clearer (see page 18).

TIP

If you are making a deeper shaped pillbox, your loops will need to be longer and wider.

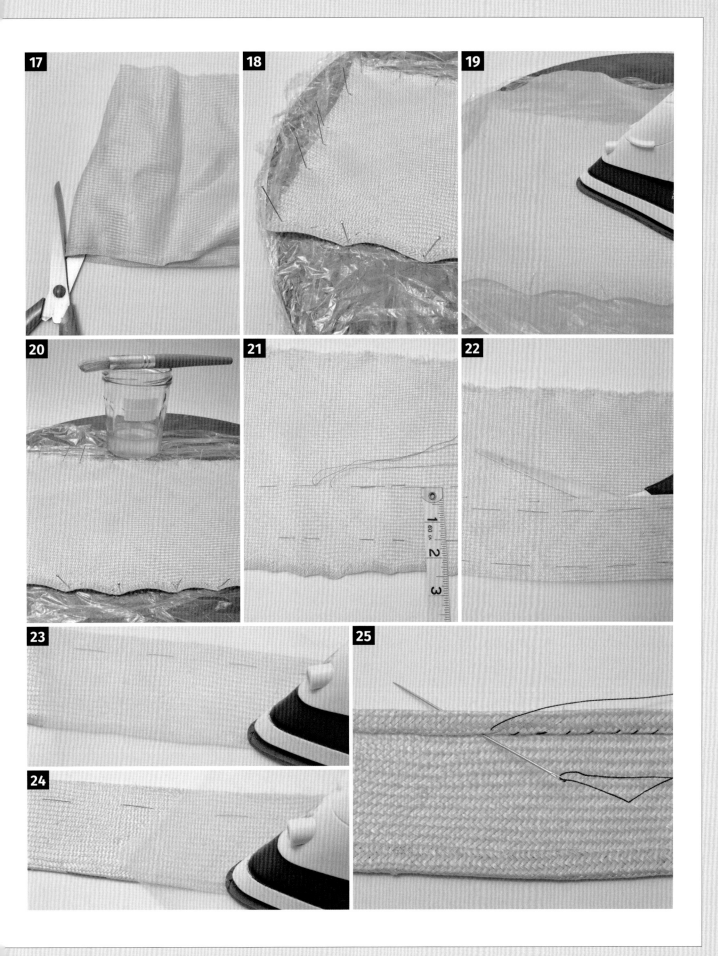

26 Fold over the ends of the straw at a right angle, with the wrong side facing up.

27 Cut off the excess, leaving a ⅜in (1cm) turned over piece.

28 Repeat steps 22, 23 and 24 to form a nice sharp end. Repeat with the other end.

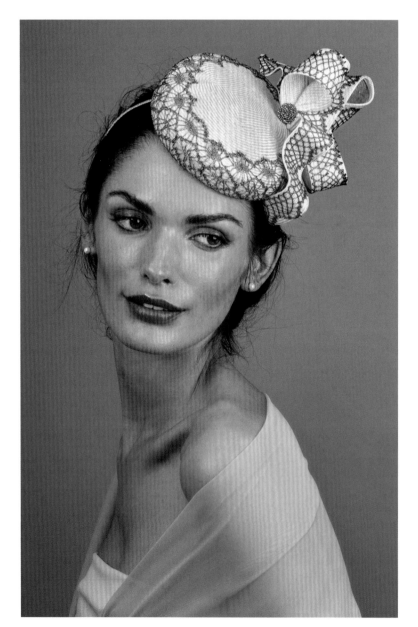

Adding the braid to the loops

29 Give the rest of your gold lace braid a press with your iron. Select a pattern in your lace and carefully cut around it to fit the width of the straw.

30 Cut a strip of adhesive web the same length and width of the straw trim, adding ⅜in (1cm) to fold over each end. Remove it from the paper and lay it on top of the right side of the straw trim.

31 Place the cut lace braid on top of the adhesive web then pin in place, folding the braid over each end to just cover the turned edge on the wrong side.

32 Press with the iron, bonding the lace braid and straw together using a pressing cloth between the iron and braid. Take out the pins.

33 Take the straw braid length, then make twists and loops and pin into a desired shape that will look attractive on the pillbox. Sew with stab stitch (see page 18) where your pins are.

34 Pin the trimming onto the pillbox shape at ten past two where the braid is joined and sew on using double cream thread and stab stitch, hiding your stitches in the folds.

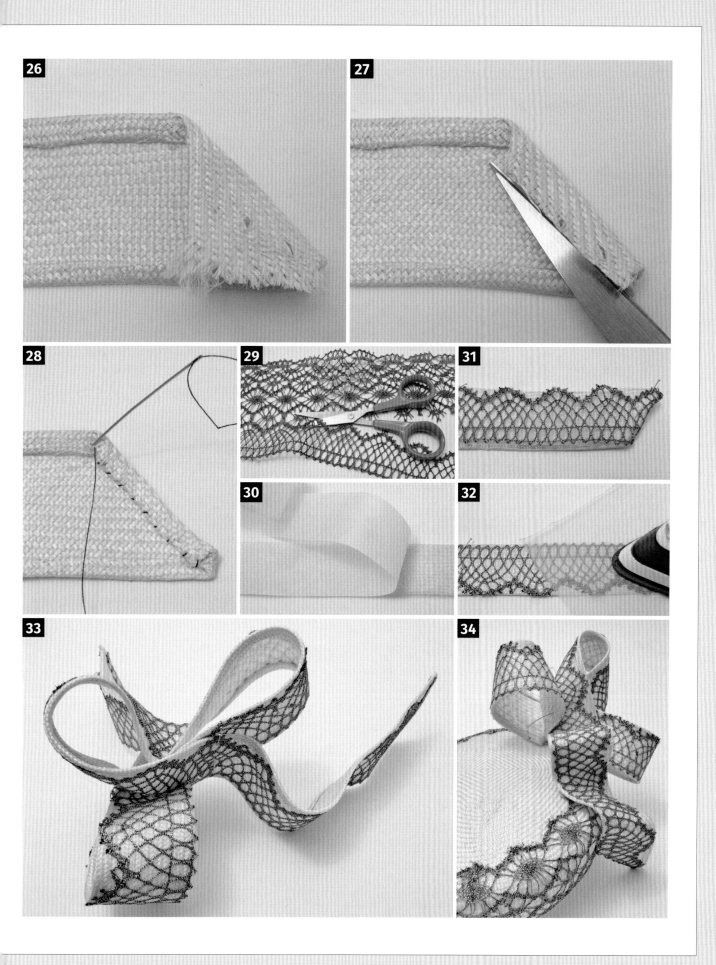

Adding the lining and Alice band

35 Make a tip and side band lining or use a gathered lining stitch (see page 32).

36 Cover the Alice band with embroidery thread (see page 34).

37 Sew your button or brooch trimming on securely in a desired position in the folds.

38 Trim off any excess straw under the petersham ribbon, leaving a ⅜in (1cm) edge.

39 Take the lining off the block and slip it into the hat, lining up the back seam with the centre back. Turn over the raw edge and pin onto the straw edge under the petersham ribbon.

40 Sew the lining in with a diagonal stitch (see page 19) with single thread small enough so the petersham ribbon hides it.

41 Sew in the Alice band so the hat sits nicely on a jaunty angle on the left of the head (see page 35).

42 You've finished!

TIP

Try the hat on your head before sewing it onto the hairband to get the desired angle.

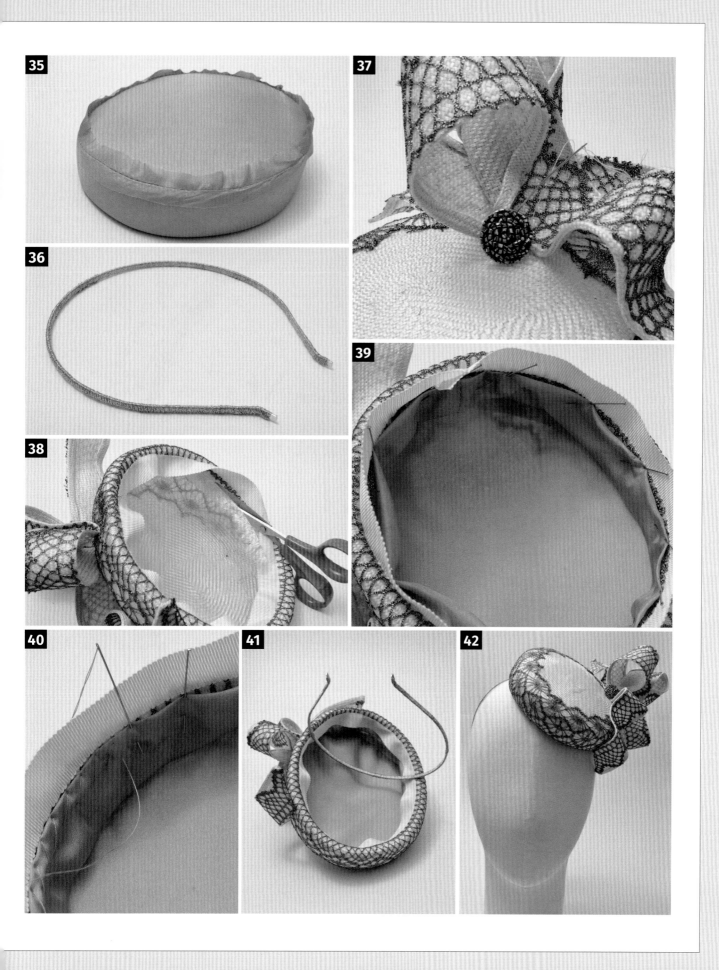

SPARKLING COCKTAIL HAT

The whimsical beauty of this piece defies its simplicity. Blocked on a polystyrene ball readily available from any good craft shop, this accessible project is a joy to make.

You will need:

4in (10cm) polystyrene ball
Bread knife
Food wrap
Water spray bottle
Brown felt-tip pen
Needles
Pins
Thimble
Brown sewing thread
Tape measure
Scissors
Pliers with a cutting edge
Iron
Curling tongs
Adhesive spray

For the hat:
8in (20.5cm) strip of pre-stiffened
    brown sinamay
8in (20.5cm) bronze sparkly fabric
16in (40.5cm) length of US 16 gauge
    (SWG 18, 1.2mm) white
    millinery wire
13in (33cm) length of no. 3 petersham
    ribbon to match bronze sparkly fabric

For the feathers and trimming:
1 brown goose quill feather
4 or 5 natural-colour curled pheasant
    quills
1 peacock feather
⅜in (1cm) bunch of black burnt peacock
    and 1 burnt pheasant feather in brown
    or black
Bronze glitter dust
Bronze colour spray
Brooch or vintage findings

For the veil, band and lining:
20in (51cm) veiling
Alice band and brown embroidery thread
    to cover
13in (33cm) bias cut strip of lining

Making the base

1 Cut the polystyrene ball in half, using a bread knife.

2 Cover the ball with food wrap so it's smooth. Take the sinamay and dampen it slightly using the water spray bottle. Pull two layers of sinamay over the ball and pin securely underneath, making sure there are no gathers anywhere and the sinamay is smooth all over. Leave to dry.

3 Colour the wire with brown felt-tip pen. Take the sinamay off the polystyrene ball and trim the raw edge down to ½in (1.5cm).

4 Using your fingers, smooth out any bumps in the wire and curve it to fit around the sinamay shape. Slip the wire into the shape and pin in place – your wire will be overlapping roughly 3in (7.5cm). Sew in using blanket stitch (see page 21).

5 Gently ease the sparkly fabric over the shape, making sure the fabric is smooth and there are no gathers. Pin the underneath edge to the sinamay.

6 Sew a diagonal stitch around the bottom edge to secure the fabric to the sinamay (see page 19). Trim the excess fabric from the sparkly fabric edge to the sinamay edge.

7 Curve the petersham ribbon and sew into the hat (see page 30), starting at the back where your wire join is.

Making the feather trimming and veiling

8 On one side of the goose quill, cut down to approx. ½in (1.5cm) width from the centre quill. Gently curve the feather, holding the quill around the heated hair tongs.

9 Spray a fine layer of adhesive spray on the goose feather and sprinkle with glitter dust. Snip the end of the stem off to the desired length.

10 Spray the peacock feather lightly with a bronze spray, trim the sides to a nice shape and cut the end of the stem so that the feather is approx. 9in (23cm) in length.

TIP
Holding feathers gently around heated curling tongs gives them a beautiful curl.

11 Cut the end of the stem on the burnt pheasant feather so that it is approx. 15in (38cm) in length. Take all the feathers except the glittered goose quill and one by one sew together at the stems by stabbing through the quills. Make a pleasing display at varying lengths and angles.

12 Mark the front of the piece by eye with a pin. Approx. 2in (5cm) to the right of the pin, sew on the bunch of feathers securely with double thread by stabbing in and out.

13 Now sew the glittered goose feather onto the front of the bunch by sewing through the quill so that it's secure.

14 Using a double thread, sew the vintage brooches/trimmings on firmly at the base of the feathers.

15 Wave the veiling in steam for a few seconds to get any creases out and cut the width down to 5in (12.5cm). Starting at the back, pin the veiling onto the base, coming roughly 2in (5cm) over the front. With single thread, sew a few tie tacks to keep the veil in place, keeping it nice and light (see page 19).

Adding a lining and band

16 Make a gathered lining (see page 33) and sew into the hat under the petersham ribbon. Cover an Alice band with brown embroidery thread (see page 35).

17 Pin and sew the Alice band onto the edge of the petersham ribbon approx. 3½in (9cm) up on the right side and 6in (15cm) up on the left side, using double thread.

18 Using the hair tongs, gently curl any feathers to your liking. You've finished!

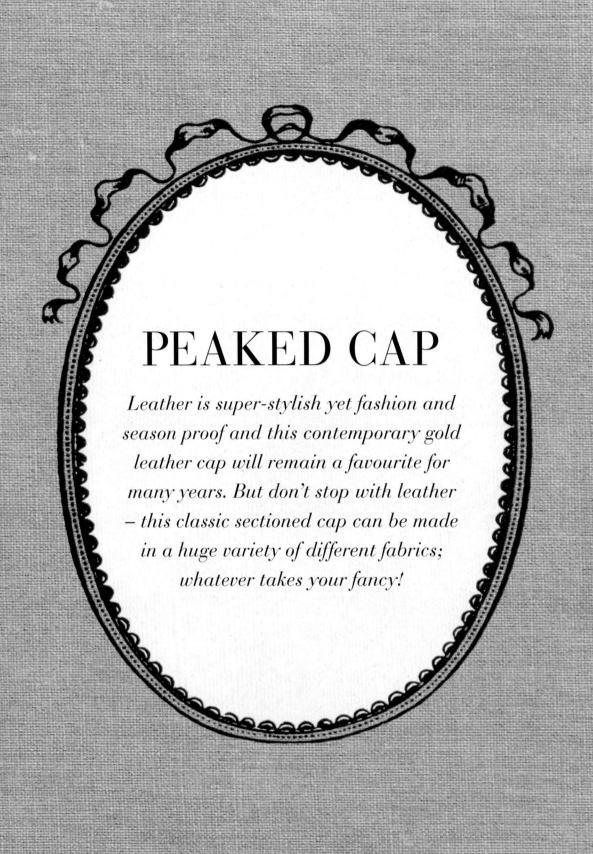

PEAKED CAP

Leather is super-stylish yet fashion and season proof and this contemporary gold leather cap will remain a favourite for many years. But don't stop with leather – this classic sectioned cap can be made in a huge variety of different fabrics; whatever takes your fancy!

You will need:

The patterns for the cap and peak
A sewing machine with the correct
    needle for sewing leather
A hand-sewing leather needle
Needles
Pins
Thimble
Sewing thread in colours to match
    chosen fabrics
Tape measure
Scissors
Small weights
Iron and ironing board
All-purpose glue

For the hat:
18in (45.5cm) foundation fabric for
    the toile
18in (45.5cm) shot satin for the lining
    (any lightweight fabric would be
    suitable)
One skin of gold leather – leather skins
    vary in size and quality so do check
    with your supplier that the skin you
    are buying is suitable for hat making
    and big enough for all the pattern
    pieces (six sections and two peaks)
17 x 5in (43 x 12.5cm) bias strip of
    medium-weight buckram
23½in (59.5cm) length of no. 5
    petersham ribbon
One self-cover button and diamanté
    to decorate it

TIP

We highly recommend making a toile before cutting into
expensive or precious fabric. And, for this project, by making a
toile not only will you be able to ensure the pattern is a correct
fit but you will also gain valuable precision and machining skills.
The toile will also serve as a foundation layer if the finished cap
needs more structure. We are using a treated curtain lining that
is lightweight but has good stiffness and body to it. A medium-
weight calico or something similar would also be suitable.

Making the toile

1 Transfer the patterns for the cap and peak
on pages 118 and 120 to paper (see page 35),
marking the bias line on the cap pieces and
the centre front notch on the peak pieces.
Cut out six of the cap pattern pieces in paper
and two of the peak. Both the cap and the
peak pattern pieces include ½in (1.5cm) seam
allowance and will make up to a cap with a
22in (56cm) head size. If you have a larger or
smaller head size you will need to alter the
pattern (see note opposite).

2 Pin the six cap pattern pieces to the
toile fabric, matching the bias line on the
pattern piece to the bias of the fabric. Mark
accurately around each piece and cut out.

3 With right sides facing, pin and machine
stitch two of the cap sections together.
Start sewing at the top of the section, using
a ½in (1.5cm) seam allowance.

4 At the top of the two stitched sections, press
open the seam with your fingers, and with
right sides facing, pin on the third section.

5 Again starting at the top of the sections,
machine stitch the third section. Put these
three joined sections to one side and repeat
the process with the other three sections.

6 Even though the toile won't be seen it will
still need to be top stitched. It will give it
strength and body, which is essential when
checking if the fitting is right and if it needs
to be used for structure in the finished
cap. We will just be top stitching the centre
sections of each half of the cap for now.
Working on the right side of the fabric, press
open the seam allowance with your fingers
and run a line of machine stitching close to
the seam all the way around the section.

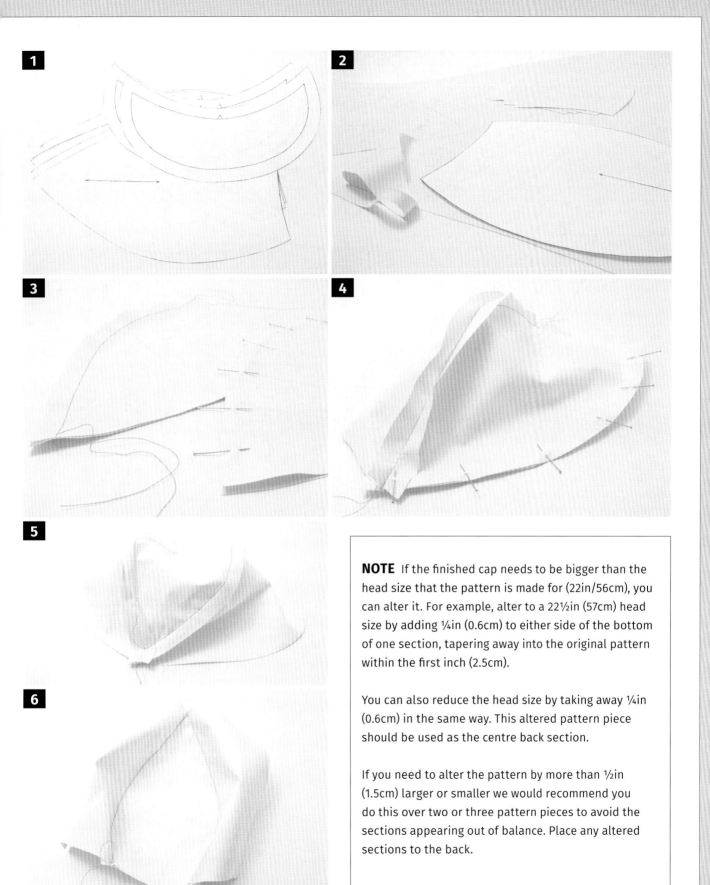

NOTE If the finished cap needs to be bigger than the head size that the pattern is made for (22in/56cm), you can alter it. For example, alter to a 22½in (57cm) head size by adding ¼in (0.6cm) to either side of the bottom of one section, tapering away into the original pattern within the first inch (2.5cm).

You can also reduce the head size by taking away ¼in (0.6cm) in the same way. This altered pattern piece should be used as the centre back section.

If you need to alter the pattern by more than ½in (1.5cm) larger or smaller we would recommend you do this over two or three pattern pieces to avoid the sections appearing out of balance. Place any altered sections to the back.

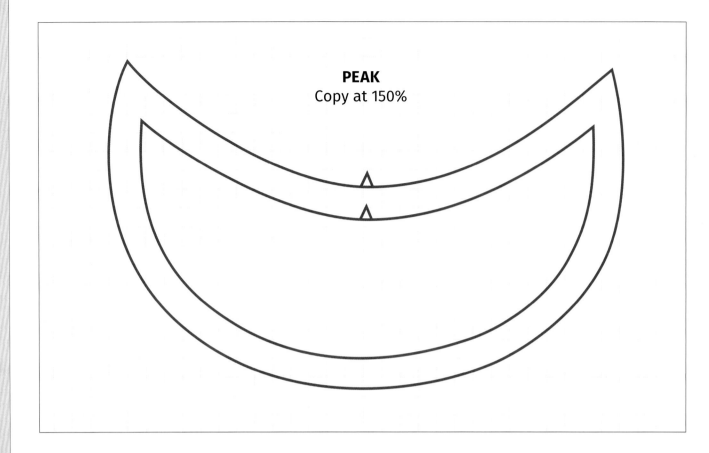

PEAK
Copy at 150%

7 Trim the seam allowance back to approx. ¼in (0.6cm).

8 Repeat the top stitching to the centre section of the other half of the cap.

9 With right sides facing, match the tops of the centre sections of both halves and pin in place.

10 Starting at the centre top, machine one side of the sections together.

11 Starting at the centre top, machine the other side together.

12 Turn the cap to the right side and top stitch the remaining four sections. Trim back all seams to ¼in (0.6cm).

Making the lining

13 It's pleasing to see beautiful fabric on the inside of a hat. We have used a shot satin for this lining but any lightweight fabric would do. Repeat steps 2–12 to make up the lining.

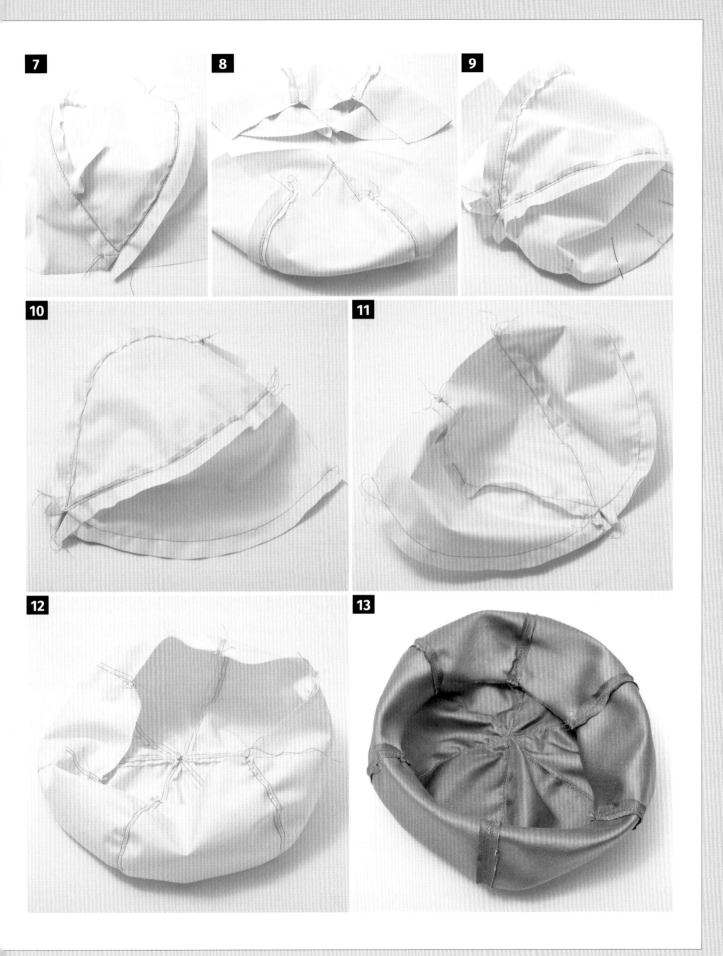

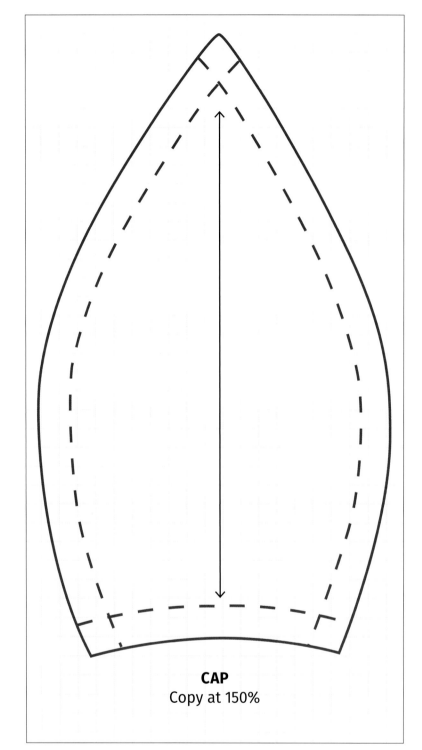

CAP
Copy at 150%

Making the outer hat

14 Lay out the six pattern pieces for the cap and the two pattern pieces for the peak on the leather in the best possible arrangement. If there are unavoidable flaws in the leather, ensure that these sections are placed to the back of the cap when making up.

15 Use small weights to keep the pattern pieces in place while cutting out, as any pins will leave permanent marks in the leather.

16 When you are cutting the peak pattern out, make sure you are using the outer line of the pattern that includes the seam allowance.

17 If you are confident using a sewing machine, you shouldn't need to pin the sections together. But if you prefer to use pins, they will need to be within the ½in (1.5cm) seam allowance, as pin marks will show in the leather.

18 Sew the leather sections together in the same way as the toile and the lining, joining three sections together then top stitching the middle sections (see steps 2–12).

19 Join the two halves together and top stitch the remaining four sections. Trim all seams back to ¼in (0.6cm).

20 Choose the centre front of the leather cap and make a front mark within the ½in (1.5cm) seam allowance.

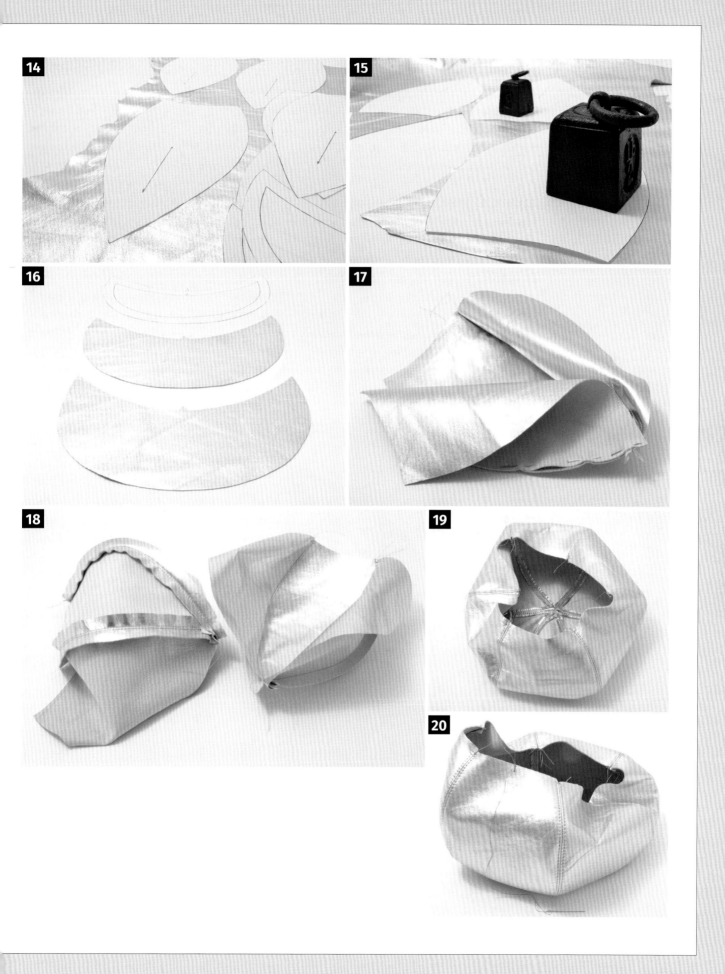

Making the peak

21 Fold the buckram strip in half so that you have one piece that is 8½ x 5in (21.5 x 12.5cm). Draw around the inner line of the peak pattern with a pencil (the inner line is the peak without any seam allowance).

22 Machine stitch the two pieces of buckram together with a few lines of stitching within the pencil lines to give the peak extra strength.

23 Cut out the peak, including the notch marking the centre front.

24 With right sides facing, sew the two cut-out leather peak pieces together, again pinning within the ½in (1.5cm) seam allowance.

25 Trim back the seam allowance to ¼in (0.6cm).

26 Make snips in the seam allowance approx. every ¼in (0.6cm). Take care not to snip right up to the sewing line.

27 Turn the leather peak pieces right side out and sandwich the buckram peak between the two layers of leather. On the right side of the peak the buckram should lie on top of the two layers of seam allowance. Pin the two layers together in the seam allowance of the inner curve of the peak and stitch with a diagonal stitch to hold them together.

28 With the right side of the peak facing in to the right side of the cap, match the centre front notch of the peak to the centre front mark on the cap and pin together.

29 Tack the peak to the cap on the ½in (1.5cm) seam allowance line.

30 Machine stitch the peak to the cap on top of your tacking line. Remove the tacking stitches.

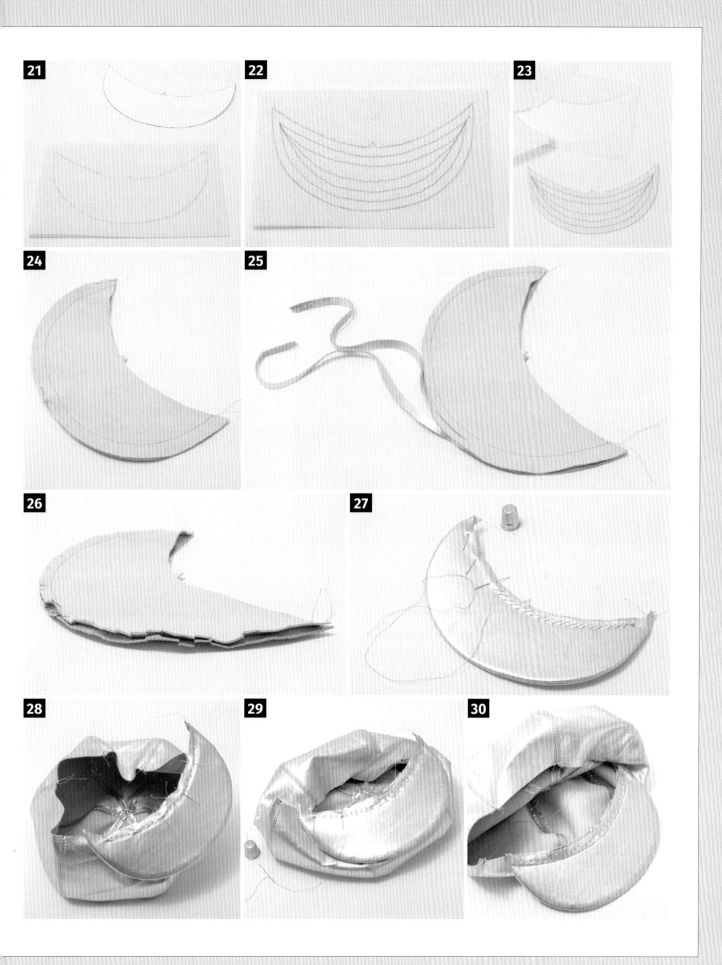

Making the button

31 Cut a piece of leather approx. ⅜in (1cm) larger than the button you are using.

32 Take out any of the back pieces from the self-covered button and cover by stitching side to side with a double thread, bringing all the leather tightly into the centre.

33 Using glue, cover the top of the button with diamanté.

34 Sew the button on to the centre of the cap.

35 Once the button is sewn on, cover the edge and any gaps with more diamanté.

Attaching the lining

36 Choose the centre front of the lining and mark with a pin. Place the lining right side facing out inside the leather cap, making sure that all the seams are lined up. Pin within the seam allowance to keep both pieces in place.

37 Tack the leather and the lining together on the ½in (1.5cm) seam allowance.

38 Measure the correct amount of petersham ribbon (see page 22). Pin then stitch in place (see page 30).

39 Tie tack (see page 19) the seam allowance under the petersham ribbon to the lining at all six seams.

40 You've finished!

TIP

The leather we have used is firm enough to not need the toile inside as well. If you are using an especially soft leather, or suede, or other fabric that needs more body to it, then sandwich the toile between the facing fabric and the lining, again matching all seams.

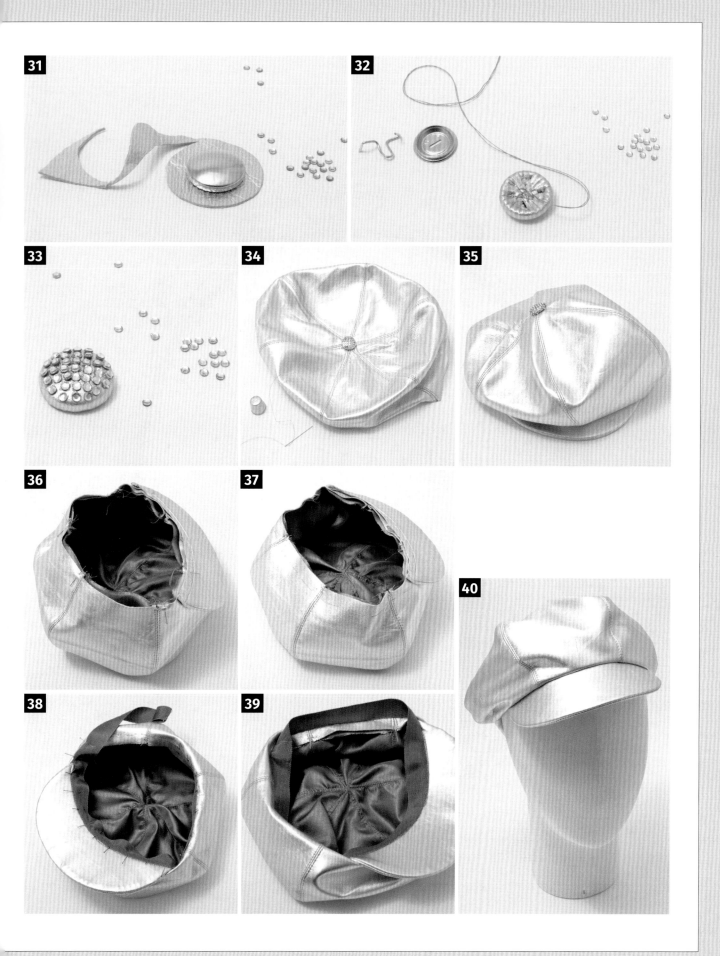

SCULPTED SINAMAY

A beautiful quality sinamay straw is hand sculpted into this dramatic shape. Trimmed with twisted feathers and organza flowers, this would be the perfect stand-out piece for any race meeting or wedding.

You will need:

The shape pattern and petal pattern
Steam iron and ironing board
Pressing cloth
Pressing pad
Pliers with a cutting edge
Needle
Pins
Thimble
Thread in natural colour
Any colour tacking thread
Thread to match silk organza
Tape measure
Scissors
Curling tongs
All-purpose glue
Firm-hold hairspray

For the hat:
17½ x 35½in (44.5 x 90cm)
    pre-stiffened good quality-grade
    natural sinamay
17 x 18in (43 x 45.5cm) veiling (or you
    can join two narrower widths together)
Approx. 60in (152cm) length of US
    16 gauge (SWG 18, 1.25mm) white
    millinery wire
Alice band and black embroidery thread
    to cover

For the roses and feathers:
Bunch of stamens
19in (48.5cm) length of US 26 gauge
    (SWG 27, 0.4mm) white millinery wire
10in (25.5cm) silk organza (we've used
    two colours)
5 side-tail pheasant feathers in black

Making the sinamay base

1 Fold the sinamay in half and press flat with a steam iron. Transfer the pattern on page 132 onto paper (see page 35) and cut out. Pin the pattern on the bias grain. Cut out two layers. Sew front and back centre marks on the inside of the seam allowance.

2 Straighten the wire to take out some of the curve (see page 26). Place it onto the pattern with the end starting at the 'V' point and curve it to follow the seam allowance shape. You can use the pointed end of the pliers to bend the four points. Your join will go up one side of the 'V' cut-out. Join the wire (see page 27).

3 Pin your wire into place along the seam allowance ¾in (2cm) in from the edge on the wrong side (underside) of the sinamay.

4 Starting at the join in the wire, sew in the wire with blanket stitch (see page 28). Stitches should be approx. 1in (2.5cm) apart and just catching a tiny piece of the sinamay so they won't be visible from the right side.

5 Place your veiling onto the right side of the sinamay so the bias is placed onto the centre front. Cut the veiling to the sinamay shape. Press flat with a steam iron. Pin in place. Sew large tacking stitches to keep the veiling flat.

6 Turn the shape over to the wrong side facing up. Bend the seam allowance over the wire edge, snipping into the V-shaped corners, then press with an iron. If you don't have enough sinamay at the bottom of the V-shape to completely cover the wire, don't worry – the flowers cover all this area. Fold over ⅜in (1cm) of the seam allowance all the way around the edge. Fold this in half again and sew down with a slip stitch (see page 19), making sure all the veiling ends are tucked in and the turning is straight and equal distance all around. Snip any surplus sinamay off when doing the corners to remove bulk for a nice sharp finish.

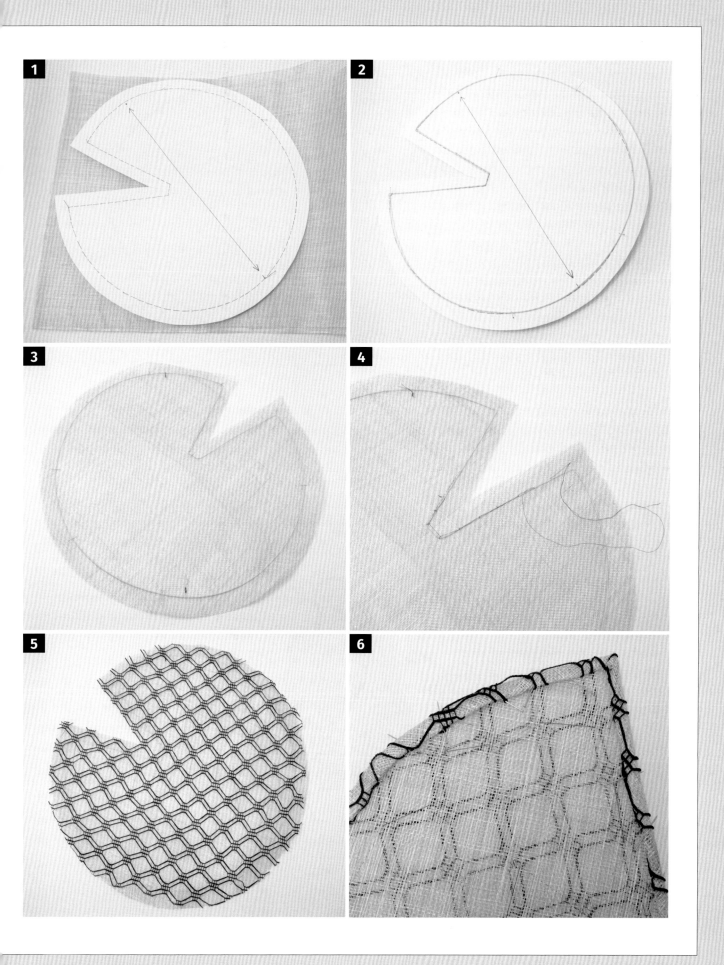

Shaping the sinamay base

7 Now place the shape right side up and with the front centre mark facing you. Start to shape and curve the edge of your sinamay following the finished photograph of the hat. As a guide, both curves at their centre on the left and right are approx. 7½in (19cm) from the centre front mark. Where the cut-out 'V'-shape is, make the bottom bit of the 'V' flat to the head and have the two sides coming up at nice angles that suit the shape on your own head. The veiling may lift up a bit from shaping the sinamay, so sew a few invisible tie tacks (see page 19) wherever needed so the veiling sits flat against the shape again. If needed also give the shape a press in the hand (see page 10).

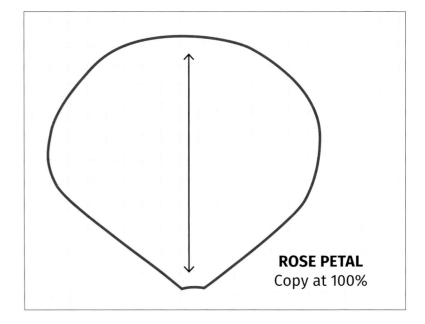

ROSE PETAL
Copy at 100%

Adding the Alice band

8 Cover the Alice band with black embroidery thread (see page 34). To obtain the correct positioning for sewing the band into the hat, measure 3½in (9cm) up on the left side of the band and 6½in (16.5cm) on the right of the band and mark the positions with pins.

9 On the sinamay shape, measure 5in (12.5cm) back from the centre front edge. Pop a pin in. Place the centre of the band onto this pin mark and pin in place. Then pin the band onto the sinamay approx. 1½in (4cm) to the left. Next measure 3½in (9cm) band to the right and pin onto the shape. Try the hat on in the mirror to ensure the correct positioning of the hat on your head and make any necessary adjustments. Using double thread, sew the band in securely with tiny stitches on the right side so they don't show. Take out the tacking stitches that were used to hold the veiling in place in step 5.

Making the roses

10 Take a bunch of stamens and knot them together in the middle with a long piece of thread.

11 Cut 5in (12.5cm) length of US 26 gauge (SWG 27, 0.4mm) wire and make a turning of ⅜in (1cm) at one end. Catch the middle of the stamens in the turning of the wire.

12 Bring the stamens together to make a bunch and wrap with thread to secure. Finish with a small blob of glue and then snip the thread.

13 Cut out eight petals for the small rose, 13 petals for the medium-sized rose and 16 petals for the large rose in both colours. Lay the petals out on paper and saturate with hairspray. Leave to dry.

14 Shape each petal by manipulating the fabric between your fingers to create dents and randomly curled edges.

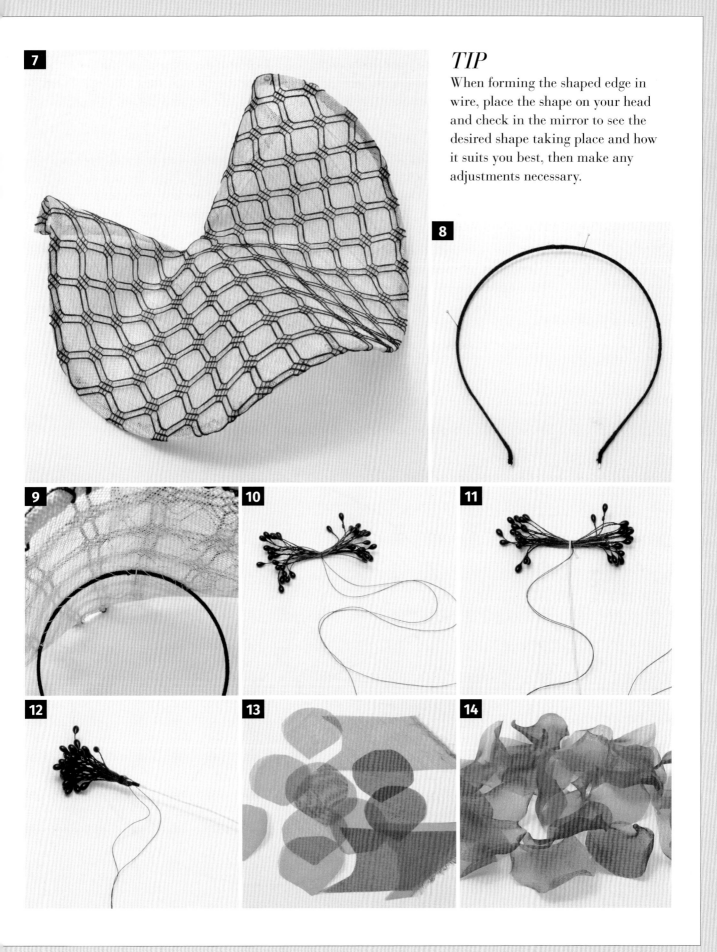

7

TIP
When forming the shaped edge in wire, place the shape on your head and check in the mirror to see the desired shape taking place and how it suits you best, then make any adjustments necessary.

8

9

10

11

12

13

14

15 To make a small rose, pick a petal and wrap it around the stamens and wire. Stitch it in place at the base of the petal with matching thread.

16 Gather the remaining part of the petal around the wire, gently folding over the top edge by approx. ⅜in (1cm). Stitch and wrap to secure it at its base.

17 Choose the next petal and place it on top of the first, but to one side, so that it starts to create the centre of the rose. Gently fold over approx. ⅜in (1cm) of the top edge of this petal too. Stitch securely to the first petal at the base of the petal.

18 Repeat this process with the next three petals for the small rose, keeping the rose shape nice and balanced and using both colours of petals.

19 Keep the stitches nice and tiny.

20 Using all-purpose glue, stick the last three petals to the base of the rose. If you feel that the rose needs to be larger and would benefit from more petals, cut out, shape and add some more.

21 Lightly spray the whole rose with hairspray to fix. Repeat steps 15–21 to make up the medium and large rose.

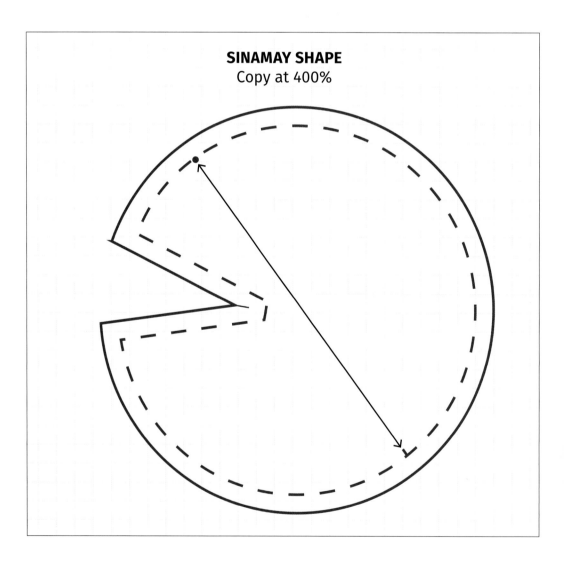

SINAMAY SHAPE
Copy at 400%

Cutting and shaping the feathers

22 Strip off one side of one of the feathers by holding the very tip of the feather in one hand and pulling down on the barbs with the other until they are stripped from the quill. With sharp scissors, snip a nice angle into the tip on the other side of the feather. Approx. 1in (2.5cm) down from the angled cut, snip in again at an angle and pull away the feather. Continue this down the entire feather to the bottom of the stem.

23 Take a second feather. Instead of stripping one side off, cut down both sides in the same way as step 22.

24 Take a third feather and this time snip in at a steeper angle to create a sharper arrow-like shape. You can snip both sides of the feather or strip one side off first.

25 With the last two feathers, cut them as you prefer, using the steps above so you have a nice collection of differently cut feathers.

TIP

When deciding where to sew on the feathers, hold the flowers in position with them initially to see how the feathers curl around them and decide what looks best.

Assembling the hat

26 Using a combination of steam and curling tongs, gently curl each feather to a pleasing shape. Snip the stem of each feather off and one by one pin and sew the feathers in place where you think looks best, using double cream thread and a stab stitch (see page 18). Don't forget to check how the back of the back of hat is looking – place one or two feathers there in positions of your choice.

27 Place the small and large roses on the front of the hat. Snip the wire stem down to roughly 1in (2.5cm). Pin the small rose to the left coming down into the curve. Pin the large rose to the right filling in the 'V'-shape. Sew on securely with cream thread using tie tacks (see page 19).

28 Pin the medium-sized rose on the back of hat and sew on in the same way as above. Let the petals of this rose spill over into any gaps and cover any places where the feathers have been sewn on. You can make up a few more petals if needed to tie tack on if you need to cover more stems. Look at the hat from all sides to make sure it looks good from every angle.

29 Take the front and back marks out and, if needed, curl the feathers with curling tongs again on the ends. You've finished!

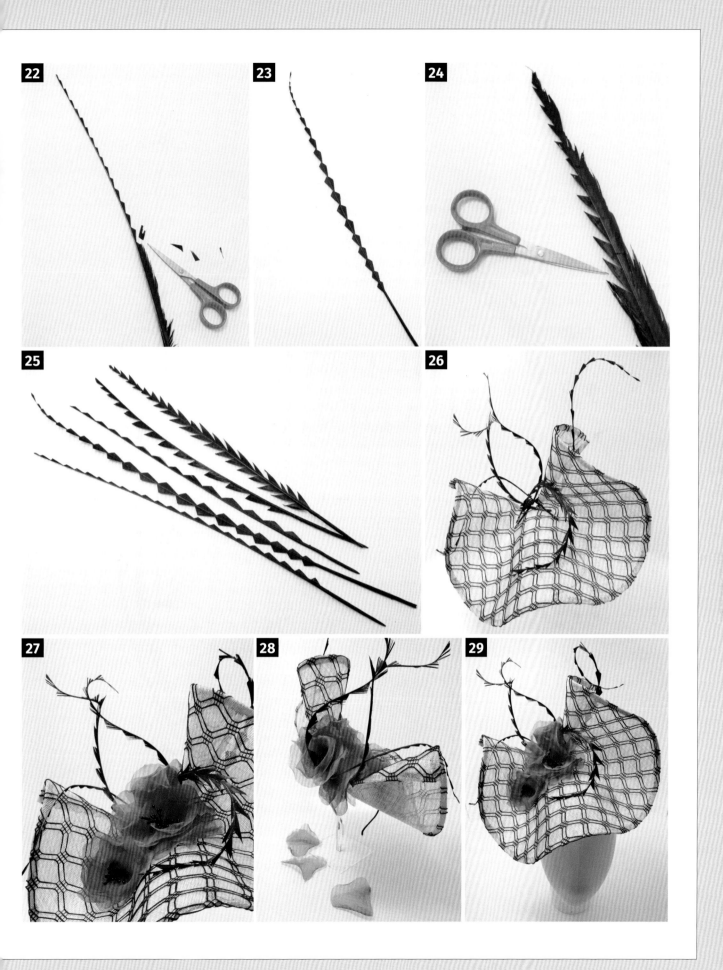

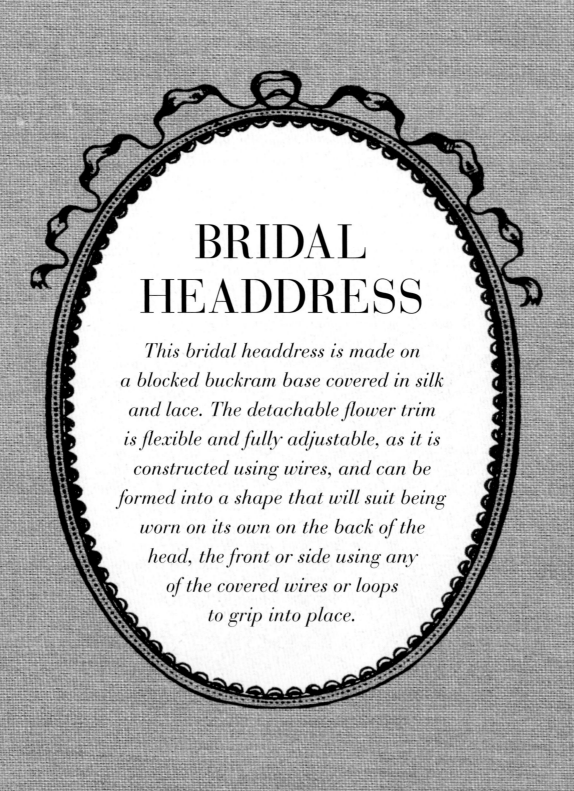

BRIDAL HEADDRESS

This bridal headdress is made on a blocked buckram base covered in silk and lace. The detachable flower trim is flexible and fully adjustable, as it is constructed using wires, and can be formed into a shape that will suit being worn on its own on the back of the head, the front or side using any of the covered wires or loops to grip into place.

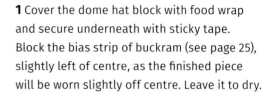

You will need:

The base pattern and petals pattern
Dome block
Food wrap
Sticky tape
Needles
Pins
Fine silk pins
Thimble
Sewing thread in colours to match fabrics
Pliers with a cutting edge
Tape measure
Scissors
Pencil
Bradawl
Iron and ironing board
All-purpose glue
Firm-hold hairspray

For the hat:
10 x 7in (25.5 x 18cm) bias strip of
    medium-weight buckram
22in (56cm) length of US 16 gauge
    (SWG 18, 1.2mm) millinery wire
10 x 7in (25.5 x 18cm) bias strip
    of domette
Two 10 x 7in (25.5 x 18cm) bias strips
    of silk dupion
10 x 7in (25.5 x 18cm) piece of lace
20½in (52cm) length of no. 3 petersham
    ribbon
Alice band and embroidery thread to cover

For the flower trim:
31 x 5in (78.5 x 12.5cm) bias strip of
    silk dupion
31 x 2½in (78.5 x 6.5cm) adhesive web
Approx. 30 x 2½in (76 x 6.5cm) strip
    of lace
1¼in (3cm) paper ball
A small selection of seed beads and/or
    small pearls
80in (203cm) length of US 26 gauge
    (SWG 27, 0.4mm) millinery wire
1 skein sliver embroidery thread

1 Cover the dome hat block with food wrap and secure underneath with sticky tape. Block the bias strip of buckram (see page 25), slightly left of centre, as the finished piece will be worn slightly off centre. Leave it to dry.

2 Transfer the base pattern on page 140 onto paper (see page 35) and cut out. Straighten and shape the wire to the outline. Transfer the front and back marks from the pattern to the wire with a pencil.

3 Join the wire with a 2in (5cm) overlap (see page 27).

4 Shape the wire to your own head shape. Gently curve the wire over the crown of the head.

5 With the buckram dry and still on the block, place the shaped and joined wire on top, ensuring the front mark on the wire is in line with the centre front of the block. Secure with two pieces of sticky tape and draw around the wire with a pencil. Mark the front and back of the buckram piece with a pencil.

6 Remove the buckram from the block and cut out following the pencil line.

7 Stitch the wire to the underside of the buckram (see page 29). The front and back marks on the wire should match up with those on the buckram. If you find the wire is a little too big or too small for the buckram shape, undo the join in the wire and adjust to fit.

8 Pin the domette onto the buckram shape. Gently pull the bias while pinning so that it lays smoothly over the buckram. Using a piece of thread, sew a back mark.

9 Trim the excess domette all around the edge back to ½in (1.5cm).

10 Stitch the domette to the buckram using a stab stitch (see page 18). Go all the way through to the right side of the piece, putting your needle back as close as possible to the same hole as it came out of so that the stitch isn't visible on the right side.

11 Cover the block with fresh, clean food wrap and block the bias strip of silk (see page 23). Lightly steam and leave to dry.

12 Lay the blocked silk over the piece and pin it in place using fine silk pins. Transfer the back mark onto the silk.

13 Keeping the pins in place, trim off the excess silk all around the edge to ½in (1.5cm). Make snips in the material at ½in (1.5cm) intervals. Keep your snips approx. ¼in (0.6cm) away from the edge of the buckram piece.

14 Stitch the silk to the domette using a diagonal stitch. Use particularly small stitches at both the points to gather and secure the material well.

15 Lay the lace over the silk-covered piece, and when you are sure of its positioning, pin in place.

16 Trim the lace leaving ½in (1.5cm) all the way round for turnings.

17 Stitch the lace to the silk using the same method as in step 14. (There will be no need to snip the lace.)

18 Pin and sew in the petersham ribbon (see page 30), making folds at both points.

19 For the lining, block the other bias strip of silk dupion in the same way as step 11.

20 Place the blocked silk inside the covered piece, pin all around the edge and cut away the excess, leaving a ½in (1.5cm) turning.

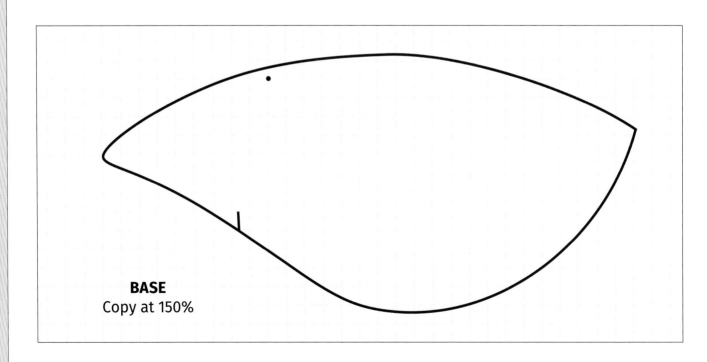

BASE
Copy at 150%

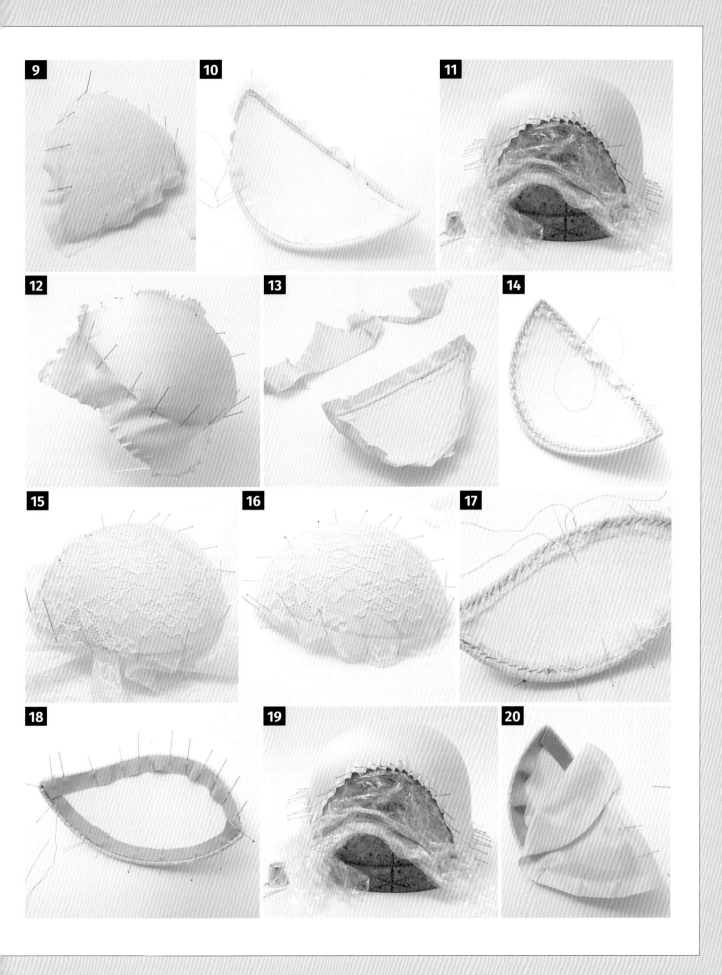

21 Slip the turning under the petersham ribbon and stitch in place, catching the silk lining to the turned-back edge of the domette and facing silk.

22 Trim back the turning so that it is all covered by the petersham ribbon.

23 Mark the covered Alice band with a pin 2in (5cm) from the bottom of one end and 4½in (11.5cm) from the bottom of the other end.

24 With the front of the piece facing you stitch the band in place (see page 35). The pin marking 2in (5cm) will be on the right and the pin marking 4½in (11.5cm) will be on the left.

Making the rose flower trim

25 Cut a 27 x 5in (68.5 x 12.5cm) bias strip of silk dupion. (This does not need to be one continuous strip.) Fold it in half and press with an iron. Cut a 27 x 2½in (68.5 x 6.5cm) strip

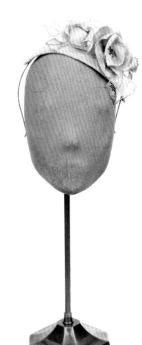

of adhesive web and sandwich it between the two layers of silk. Press according to the instructions on the adhesive web.

26 Cut out six petals using the petal pattern below as well as one bud petal and four small bud petals.

27 Using the adhesive web, cover four of the petals, one bud petal and two small bud petals with lace.

28 Using one of the petals without lace, make a gentle fold approx. one third of the way down from the top of the petal and wrap it around itself to form the centre of the rose. Secure with a stitch at the bottom and, using the same thread, fill the centre with seed beads and pearls.

29 Sew a lace-covered petal to the base of the first one, but opposite, to start building the rose into a nice rounded shape.

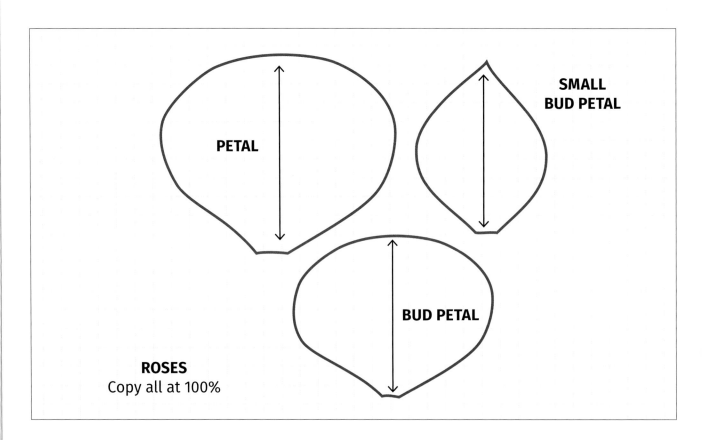

PETAL

SMALL BUD PETAL

BUD PETAL

ROSES
Copy all at 100%

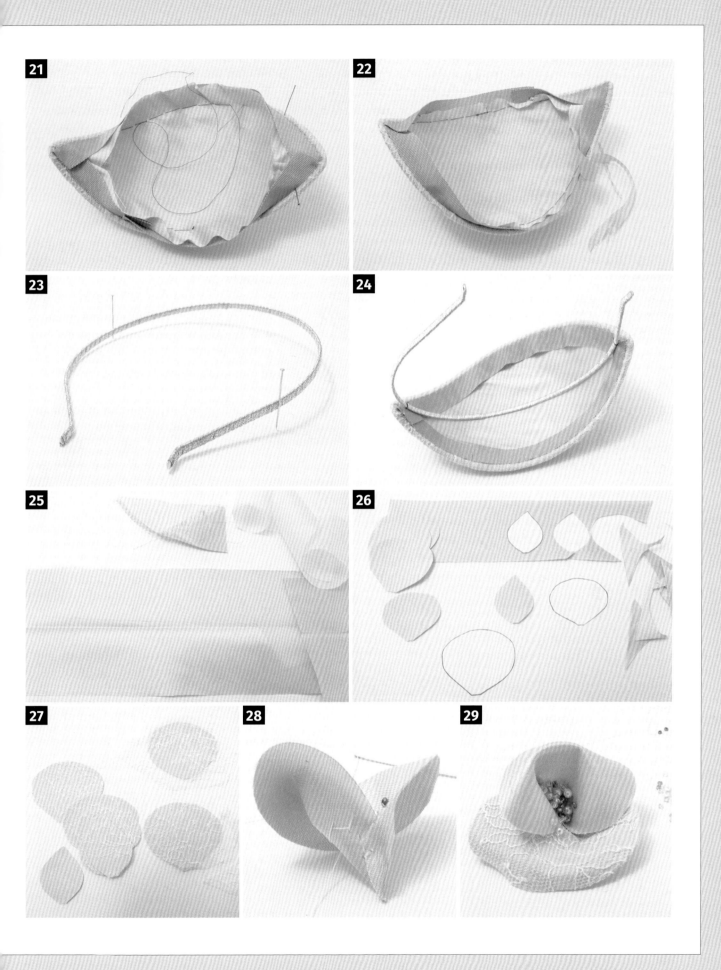

30 Continue to build the flower by sewing the other petals to the base, keeping it symmetrical. The layers of fabric at the base will get tough to sew through so you will need your thimble. If need be, stick the last couple of petals on with glue.

Making the bud

31 Cut 5in (12.5cm) of wire and wrap with embroidery thread using the same method as covering a metal Alice band (see page 34). Make a hole up through the centre of the paper ball with a bradawl. Put a blob of all-purpose glue on one end of the wire and push it up into the ball and leave to dry.

32 Cut a 4in (10cm) square of silk and cover the ball by stitching and wrapping with a double thread at the base of the ball. Keep the gathers as evenly spread out as possible.

33 Trim away the excess fabric close to the thread.

34 Stick the four small bud petals and the bud petal to the base of the covered ball, covering up the gathers and trimmed-back fabric. Spray the whole bud with hairspray to fix.

Making the leaves

35 Cut five 15in (38cm) lengths of US 26 gauge (SWG 27, 0.4mm) wire. Wrap the wires with embroidery thread, leaving approx. ¼in (0.6cm) of the wire free of thread top and bottom and approx. 1in (2.5cm) of spare embroidery thread top and bottom.

36 Using the patterns on pages 144 and 146 as a guide for the five leaf shapes, make a bend in the wire. This will be the central vein of the leaf.

37 Using pliers, make little notches in the wire as you work up towards the top of the central vein to give the impression of a leaf with serrated edges.

38 Bring the two wires together at the top of the central vein.

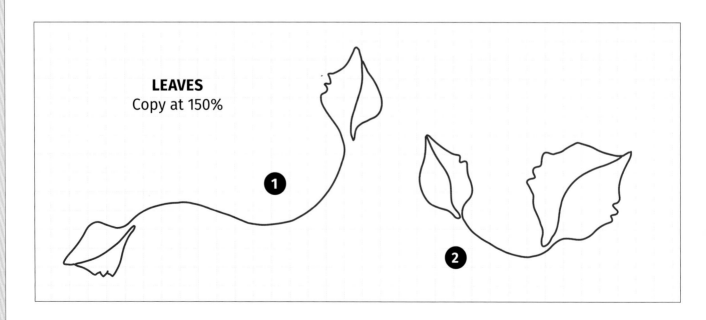

LEAVES
Copy at 150%

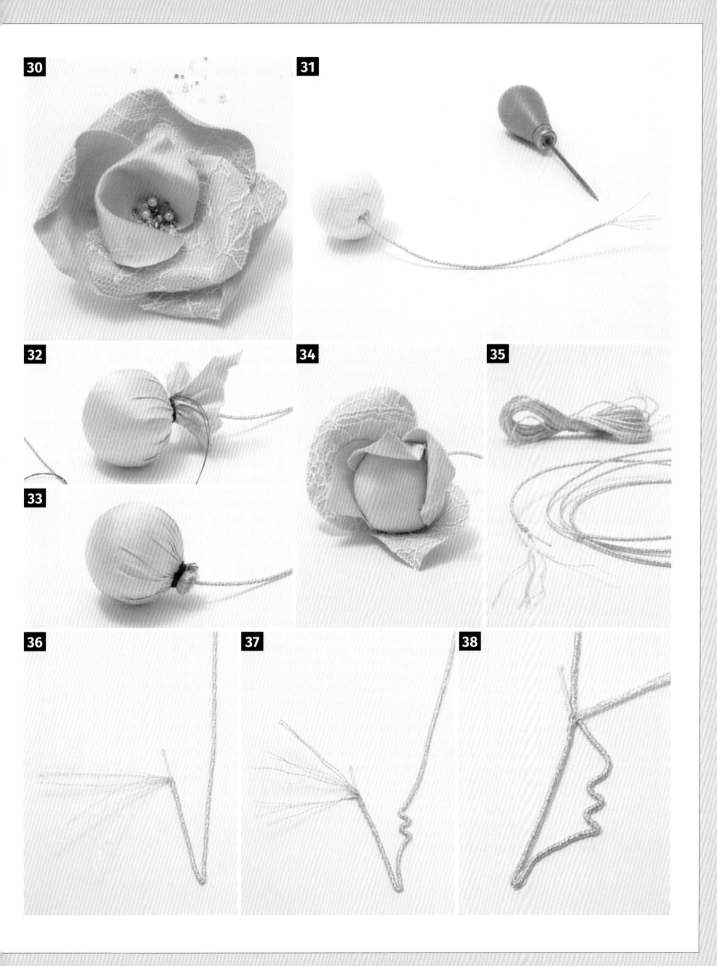

30

31

32

34

35

33

36

37

38

39 Join the two wires by gluing and wrapping with the spare embroidery thread.

40 Work back down the other side of the leaf towards the stem, again making notches, to form a complete leaf shape.

41 Cover the leaves with the lace and the silk by applying a thin layer of glue to the underneath side of the wire shape then placing it directly onto the fabric.

42 Allow the glue to dry before cutting away the excess with sharp scissors as close to the wire as possible.

43 Make a wire loop at the end of the single leafed wire by bringing the wires together and wrapping and gluing using the excess embroidery thread as in step 39. This loop will be for putting a hairgrip in to keep the headdress on the head.

44 Using the leaf assembly diagram on page 148 as a guide, shape the leaves and wires.

LEAVES
Copy at 150%

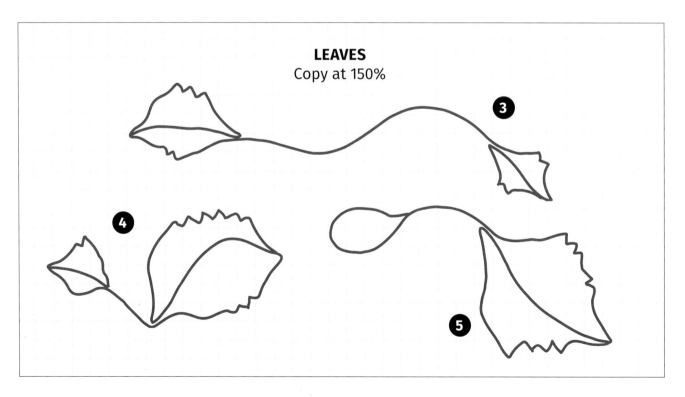

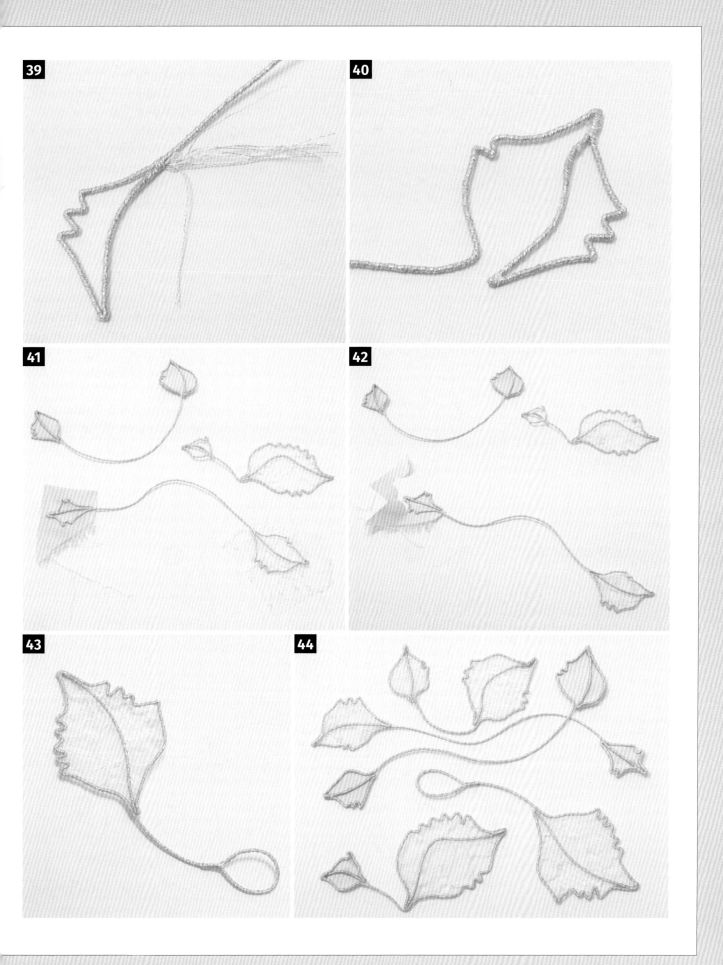

Putting it all together

45 Stitch the rose to the wire of the bud approx. 2in (5cm) from the bud's base. Use small and neat stitches and finish off the thread securely. You will probably need your thimble, as the base of the rose is quite tough to sew through.

46 Join wire number 1 to the bud wire near to the base of the bud by wrapping and knotting with thread.

47 Add wires 2 and 3 to the same place.

48 Join wires 4 and 5 in the same way but near to the base of the rose.

49 Make another loop for attaching to the head out of the end of the wire that belongs to the bud (as in step 43). To give the joins extra strength and neaten the piece at the back, cover the joining threads by wrapping and gluing with embroidery thread.

50 Arrange the leaves from the front as in the photograph, or make adjustments as you wish.

51 To attach the flower headdress to the base, use a double thread and over sew the wires of the headdress securely, going all the way through the head piece. Use stitches that can easily be snipped for when you want to wear the flower headdress on its own.

52 Make adjustments to the wires of the rose bud and leaves as you wish. You've finished!

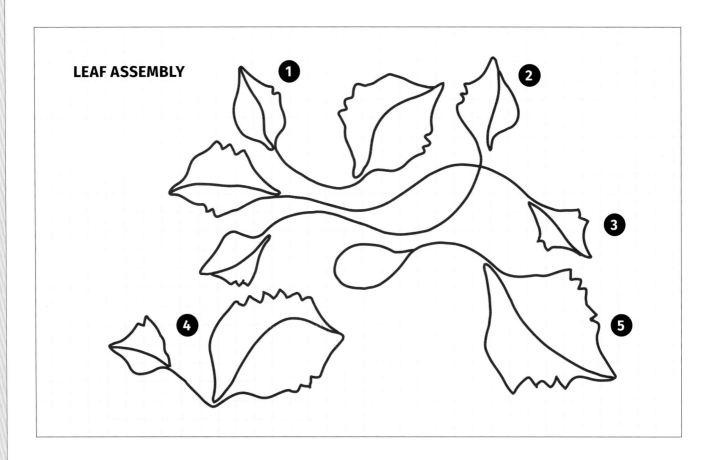

LEAF ASSEMBLY

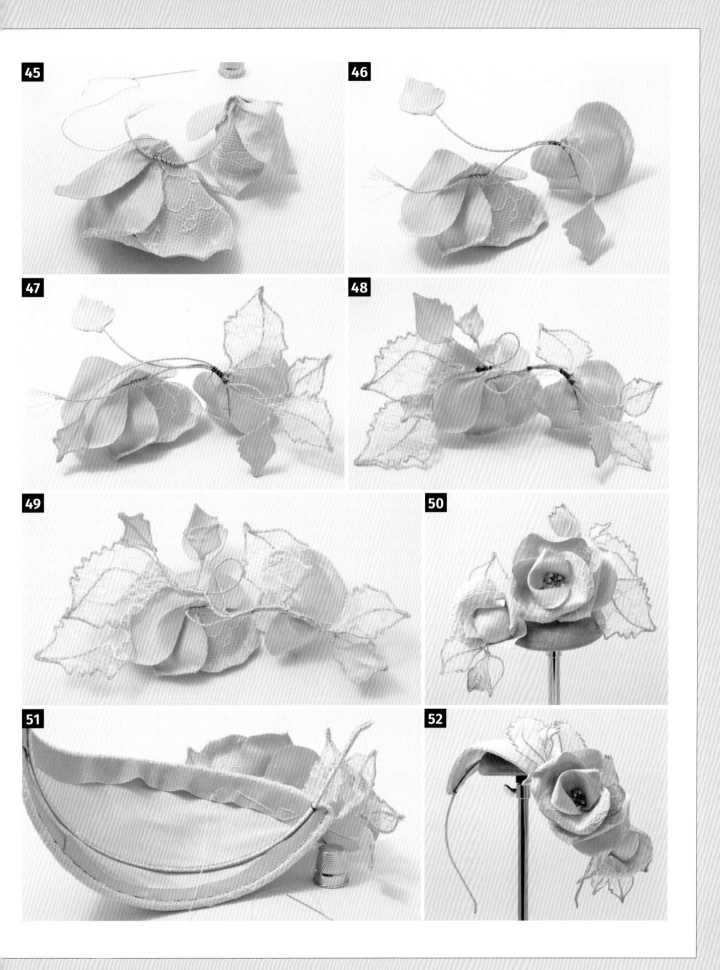

SUPPLIERS

UK SUPPLIERS RECOMMENDED BY LOMAX & SKINNER

Baxter Hart & Abraham Ltd
141 New Bedford Road
Luton, LU3 1LF
E: Hornbha@aol.com
W: baxterhart.co.uk

Hat Blocks Direct
Paul Cox
88 Acres Road
Quarry Bank
Brierley Hill
West Midlands, DY5 2XY
E: jamescox@hatblocksdirect.co.uk
W: hatblocksdirect.co.uk

Macculloch and Wallis
25-26 Poland Street
London W1F 8QN
E: mailorder@macculloch.com
W: macculloch-wallis.co.uk

Parkin Fabrics
Unit E, Prince of Wales Business Park
Vulcan Street
Oldham, OL1 4ER
E: info@parkinfabrics.co.uk
W: parkinfabrics.co.uk

Petershams Millinery Supplies
Unit 12a, The Artworks
Elephant Road
London, SE17 1AY
E: hello@petershams.com
W: petershams.com

The Silk Route
Cross Cottage
Cross Lane
Frimley Green
Surrey, GU16 6LN
E: hilary@thesilkroute.co.uk
W: thesilkroute.co.uk

The Silk Society
44 Berwick Street
London, W1F 8SE
E: sales@thesilksociety.com
W: thesilksociety.com

ACKNOWLEDGEMENTS

Sarah and Rachel would like to thank their families for their patience and support, and everyone at GMC Publications for giving them the opportunity to write this book and for guiding them through the process.

GMC Publications would like to thank:
Neal Grundy for the fashion photography and Wayne Blades for styling, Lindsey Poole for hair and make-up. Model: Justina at Zone.

INDEX

To order a book, or to request
a catalogue, contact:

GMC Publications Ltd
Castle Place, 166 High Street,
Lewes, East Sussex,
BN7 1XU
United Kingdom
Tel: +44 (0)1273 488005
www.gmcbooks.com